17 Questions – What do You think?

By Charles F. Roost, D.C.

Copyright© 2012

Acknowledgements:

I am very grateful to Bill Waltz, and Duane and Julie Feldpausch for their gracious wisdom and insights into this book. While none of them necessarily agree with all of my answers to the seventeen questions, they each took the time to, not only read, but add their thoughts to mine.

I also want to thank my wife, Judi, for her input into this book, as well as into my life. She is a wonderfully sensitive and wise, godly person without whom I would be lost and confused. An encourager, a mirror, full of the Word and the Spirit of God.

Another word of thanks to Titus Merriam, who has been a good sounding board, as well as a patient designer of my covers.

17 Questions – What do You think?

Contents

Introduction – Diamond Hard Questions – Carbon Fiber Answers
    Page 6
Chapter One – Is there anyone out there? Hello!
    Page 13
Chapter Two – Who is God? What is He like?
    Page 29
Chapter Three – The hand is quicker than the eye!
    Page 39
Chapter Four –Options in Origins
    Page 45
Chapter Five – All the souls in the universe.
    Page 62
Chapter Six –Is free will really free?
    Page 69
Chapter Seven – Is God really in control?
    Page 76
Chapter Eight – The good. The Bad. And the really, really ugly.
    Page 82
Chapter Nine – How could He?
    Page 86
Chapter Ten – Pearly gates, and lakes of fire.
    Page 91
Chapter Eleven – I don't care. Yer outa there!
    Page 95
Chapter Twelve –Can't they all be right?
    Page 103
Chapter Thirteen – When is 'nice' not nice enough.
    Page 109
Chapter Fourteen -- Please, God! Pullleeeese?!?
    Page 118

Chapter Fifteen – "Nothin' up my sleeve!"
    Page 125
Chapter Sixteen – The bent balance.
    Page 129
Chapter Seventeen – Why does any of it matter, anyway?
    Page 134
Conclusion
    Page 138

17 Questions – What do You think?

By Charles F. Roost, D.C.

Copyright © 2012 by Charles F. Roost, D.C.
Lansing, Michigan, USA

Cover design by Merriam Marketing

All rights reserved. No portion of this book may be reproduced without written permission by the publisher or author.

Published in the United States of America by DC Publishing

ISBN 978-1480287662

722 N. Creyts Rd.
Lansing, MI 48917
DrRoost@yahoo.com

Introduction –

Diamond Hard Questions – Carbon Fiber Answers

Life is not easy. There are not many who would argue with this statement. Yet, the fact that life is not easy forces us to ask some critical questions and observations. Sticky questions. Questions that are sticky in the sense that, once you start trying to answer them, they drag you deeper and deeper into their gooey depths. Many of these questions concerning the meaning of life are convoluted, and lead us from one strand of reasoning to another. They can't be separated from one another. They lead us into a maze of reasoning that is often hard to untangle. Their answers and implications impact one another in such a way that you can't truly answer one without answering others. Sticky questions, indeed.

Many of these questions are hard – diamond hard. Yet they must be answered, for some of these questions form the bedrock of what we believe about the world, about who we are, where we are going, and the meaning of life itself. Did I mention that these are hard questions?

In nature, the element Carbon, number 12 on the periodic chart, is among the most amazing of all elements. This simple atom, comprised of 6 Protons, 6 Neutrons and 12 Electrons, can be formed into the most amazing of compounds. Everything from DNA to slime is made, in various combinations with other elements, from Carbon. Even in its pure form, Carbon, all by itself, is fashioned into a wide range of materials as different as Coal, Diamonds and manmade materials like carbon fiber. Of all the materials known to man, Diamond is the hardest substance, and carbon fiber is, weight for weight, one of the strongest, yet most flexible.

Carbon fiber is also a formulation of almost entirely carbon atoms. To arrive at this molecular structure, the carbon atoms have been heated to about 2000 degrees Fahrenheit in order to align the strings of carbon atoms into a linear arrangement. These microscopic strings are then woven together into mutually-strengthening micro-yarns, and fashioned into many different products that are heat resistant, and very strong under torsion, bending, and stretching stresses. Like this man-made material, our answers should not be cumbersome, fragile or unable to hold up under examination. Like carbon fiber, our answers must be flexible, and resistant to being pulled apart.

Thus, the title of this introduction. The questions we will address are hard. As hard as diamond, and as hard as the lives lived in the face of them. The answers we crave must be equally tough, yet flexible enough to stand under the pressures and stresses of this hard life in which we find ourselves immersed.

Here is a partial list of questions that demand answers, and yet which have not been easily answered in all of the history of mankind:

- What is the right religion?
- Who is God? What is He like?
- Where did we come from?
- How can man's choices matter in the face of an "all powerful" God?
- Is there really such a thing as evil in the world?
- How can a loving God allow disasters to happen?
- How can a loving God send people to hell?
- Is God really in control?
- How does prayer work?
- How does the spiritual world impact the physical?

- Why do bad things happen to good people?
- Does my life really matter?

These are not easy questions. In fact, if there is an analogy that fits, our diamond hard description may be it. Yet they demand fair discussion, and honest reflection. For if a hard life is to make sense, if the challenges in which we find ourselves are to have meaning, these questions must have answers. And the answers at which we arrive must be real enough, and strong enough to carry the thoughtful questioner through the difficult times in life. When the storms of life come, the answers must be flexible enough to take the strain, and tough enough to last. The answers must be carbon fiber tough.

As for the accuracy or error of our answers, we must wonder if there is such a thing as a "right answer" to these questions. Our current, 'tolerant' culture would have us believe that all answers are equal. But surely some must be more accurate than others. For instance, various people do sincerely follow many different religions, fully expecting their beliefs to carry them through challenging lives and into heaven. However, some of these various religions directly contradict one another.

Concerning the debate over creation versus evolution, life did ultimately have a beginning, and not all theories of that origin can be right.

When we ponder the importance of our individual lives, our decisions do seem to matter – they impact our own life and the lives of others around us.

Does an all-powerful God cause disasters to occur? We do witness horrible events around us in the form of acts of nature and acts of man. These things occur in a world that purportedly is under the control of a good and powerful God. Yet bad things do happen to good people, even people who claim to be God's children.

Is there actually a whole spiritual dimension, just outside of our sight, that impacts our physical universe? There do seem to be things that happen in life that cannot be fully described by material events.

These observed events, and others like them, beg questions of "Why?" "How?" and "Who is right?" that we try to avoid because there seem to be no easy answers, and the discussion of them all too often leads to defensive positioning and anger rather than an attempt to reach truth.

These are the questions, the diamond hard questions that we will explore in this book. The answers at which we arrive may not make you happy at first. But we will discuss them, just the same. And if we are intellectually honest, if we come without deciding beforehand what our answers will be, we may arrive at a center of peace. We may just find enough answer to get us through. For we are going through – through a life that is often perplexing. Yet even if the life is extremely difficult at times, it does not need to be a life that is also confusing.

These questions, and the difficulties that engender them, are real. But we have a responsibility and a choice as intelligent beings. Without exception, every one of us must choose to either avoid answering the questions and to let them drag us down, or to dig in, find answers that hold water, and live in peace with the answers. When we do this, we use the answers, and even the process we go through to find the answers, to strengthen us and to remind us that we have not yet arrived at perfection, or complete understanding.

For indeed, we are not in heaven yet. And until we get there, there will be questions, we will encounter difficulties, and there will times when we wonder 'why?' There will be questions that seem unanswerable. And because some questions may not have complete answers, it makes it all the more important that we have useable answers to as many of the hard questions as we can. Having a workable foundation under as many of the diamond hard questions as possible, makes it easier to be calm in the face of unanswerable ones.

And because these unanswered questions remain, we are faced with another choice – among the sticky questions, how will we build our life? On cynicism and doubt? Or on faith in the fact that, even with all these questions and difficulties, God is still good?

With all these questions begging us for attention, where do we start? Each is an important question. Each impacts us in the heart – right where we grapple for meaning and reason. But we must start somewhere. And it turns out that the order of questions is important. Each, in a way, builds on the others. So answering the first question first is going to be important.

Therefore, we will address a foundational question first. I hesitate to do this because this question hits an area that carries presupposition to its apex. Entire sciences, political empires, world wars, and the course of history over and over, have been built on the mindset of the answer to this question. Debating this question is one of the two critical topics we were taught to avoid if you want to keep a conversation polite – politics and religion.

To make it even more harrowing to dive into this topic, it is pretty clear that every person on the face of the planet has decided on their answer to this question before they became an adult. And changing the answer after that point of decision takes, not an act of congress, but an act of God. Literally.

Have you ever noticed that some decisions are made at such a deep, emotional level, that logic and reason will rarely make a difference in it? An example is when a child is abused by a parent. The scars that occur from these experiences are so deeply rooted that their perception of what love is, and how love is expressed, is skewed from normal. It will impact their relationships, their impression of God, and their world view for years to follow. Years of counseling may make no dent in these perceptions. In such cases, only God can heal the wounds and normalize the emotional impact on that person's relationships.

In the same way, our world view is rooted deeply in our early psychological makeup. And the way you answer this basic question of world view will impact every one of the ensuing topics on our list of sticky questions – in effect dictating their answers. Truly, if you know how any person answers this question, you can predict how they will answer many of the others.

So, before you read any further, agree with me that you will think rather than react to the discussion. Come with an open mind. Come with logic, rather than emotion. Come seeking truth, rather than looking to support what you already believe. Examine the evidence and arrive at a deeper understanding of truth, rather than filtering the evidence in an effort to confirm your presuppositions.

Of course, others have addressed these questions. Greater minds than mine have sorted through the philosophical background of these issues. I think of Francis Schaefer, Clive

Staples Lewis, Dietrich Bonheoffer, and others, and while I honor their mental capacities, I sometimes tire at wading through their weighty tomes of analysis and logic.

They are giants of intellect, and I will not attempt to compete with their work. But I do desire to write in simple language, and to answer some of these questions in a way that is easy to wrap our minds around, and easy to digest and to make a part of our world view. I have no degree in theology, logic, or homiletics. But with these carbon fiber answers in place, life makes sense to me. The diamond hard questions no longer throw me. The answers work together in such a way that they give a foundation to life's challenges, twists and turns, and storms, and I hope to share them with you.

Enough said. Let us dive in. The waters are deep, but with wisdom lent from God, we can expect to have answers. I have selected seventeen sticky questions that seem to get asked often enough, but get answered with a shrug of the shoulder, a twist of the lip, and more questions. Often the questions are politely deflected. Sometimes the discussions quickly devolve to stony silence, if not anger and broken relationships. These are diamond hard questions. They demand answers if we hope to live our lives with consistency and meaning. The answers I will propose will be strong enough to hold up to scrutiny, and flexible enough to stand the stresses and tests of debate.

Let us heat the carbon atoms of data in the furnace of logic, and spin them into answers of strength and resiliency – carbon fiber answers to the hardest of questions.

Chapter One – Hello! Is there anyone out there?

Is there a God, and does He interact with humanity on any meaningful level?

Each person's world view is the infrastructure of their mental, emotional and logic filter set. Each of us has a world view. Every single one of us has, at some point in our life, made a decision about how we think the world works. Many of us never consciously think about it, but it is there, sifting the information our senses take in. Many of us don't realize we have such a filter and, if asked, "What is your world view?" we might not even know what was meant by the question. But our world view is there. It is deep in our thought processes and it impacts the way we think, the decisions we make, the kind of life we live, the kinds of friends we make, the way we look for answers in life, the way we raise our children, and the level of contentment we will find at the end of our lives.

So what is meant by our world view? And how does it affect the sticky questions in life? Our world view is the foundation of how we think. It is the basis for how we view life. The answer to each of life's difficult questions is based on our world view, so it is imperative that we consciously decide on this issue. If we are not proactive about this, if we fail to think through the question, a world view will become seated in our minds anyway. It will subtly take root in our mind and drive our decisions from that time on.

Our world view is based on our answer to the question, "Is there a God, and does He care about me?" Take a moment and think about what you believe about this question. Then write your answer down.

It is important to answer both parts of the question. It is too easy to answer the first part with a pious 'yes', and then live like that profound truth makes no difference. So go on to consider the second half of the question. Does this Supreme Being have any interest in me and my life?

Next, think back to where that answer came from. Why do you believe what you believe about that? In many cases, we don't know why we believe such a fundamental tenet. We just have always thought that way. Experts tell us that we are the way we are because of our genetic makeup and because of what we learned and how we were treated when we were 3 years old and younger. We believe what we believe about this topic because of how our parents believed, or in reaction to their beliefs, or due to traumas during upbringing, or from a lack of nurture, more than because we searched for and arrived at a logical conclusion about it.

It is also probably true that we will not change how we believe about those foundational concepts unless we deliberately dig into the facts, we encounter a massive stress that forces a change, or God changes our hearts on the matter.

Now let us back up a step and pick apart the question, so you can decide anew what you really believe what is true about this. Not what your parents said was true. Not what was seared into your heart by a painful event in your past, but what is really true. Because what you believe about this will affect your life, and your eternal destiny.

The question is, in its most basic form – is there a God? I would suggest to you that the evidence is overwhelming that there is. Let us consider preconceptions for a moment.

The scientist that has a world view of "there is no God" will look at data, point, and say, "See. There is no God." He will ignore evidence to the contrary, such as gaps in the fossil record, contradictions with laws of physics, and age of the universe issues. His world view filters all evidence, and retains only those data that reinforce his conclusion that there is no God. But taken with an open mind, the evidence actually proves that there is a God – the universe as we know it cannot work without the input of an outside intelligence.

In any investigation or search for truth there are two types of proof:

- Eyewitness
- Evidential preponderance

Of course there is no eyewitness proof of creation. No one now living was there. The closest thing we have is Moses' writings found in Genesis – the first book of the Bible. We have a similar problem with eyewitness proof of God's existence. The few people who say they have seen God face to face, lived many centuries ago. They wrote about their experiences in the books that make up our Bible, and their testimony is overwhelming in their conclusion that there is indeed a God.

There are forty different human authors of the book we now widely accepted as the Bible. Almost every one of these men had an experience that could not be explained by any other manner. Some of the authors claimed to have actually seen God. All of them testify that indeed there is a God. So among that small, but credible group, the question of God's existence is settled.

That leaves us with evidential preponderance. And what we cover in the next few paragraphs will build a strong case for evidential preponderance in favor of God's existence, of the veracity and reliability of the Bible, and of original creation by that same God.

Within our category of evidentiary preponderance there are actually two sources – the data we gather from studying the universe, and the Bible itself.

The universe, being highly organized and specifically tuned to the needs of its own continuation, must have an organizing intelligence behind its existence. There is simply no way this amazing, intricately balanced construct could have happened just from chance – no matter how long the atoms of the universe have had to randomly collide and build into more complex forms.

There are many attributes of our world, the solar system, the universe, as well as physical properties of chemistry and physics, that are so finely balanced, in precisely the way they need to be in order to allow life to exist. It could be argued that a master designer set it all up in just such a way as to allow us to exist. If any one of these hundreds of factors were off by just a small amount, in either direction, life would cease to exist. This is called the anthropic principle.

Here are some examples.

Water is a compound that we take for granted, yet it is absolutely essential for life on earth. It is needed, not only for our own life as biological beings, but for every life form on the planet as well. And, while we take it for granted in advanced countries, it is not so plentiful, nor so clean and safe, in other countries. Yet it is the physical properties of water that I want to point out in the context of our sticky question.

Water is made up of three atoms – two hydrogen molecules and one oxygen molecule. The fascinating thing about this combination is that it becomes one of the very VERY few compounds that are in liquid form at just the right temperatures to support life on earth. Even more interesting is the fact that water has factors that make it the perfect liquid to preserve life here in other ways, too. It is an ideal heat sink, a factor of its "specific heat" characteristic that allows fluctuations in temperature without boiling away or freezing the oceans into a solid, earth-sized ice cube. Water vapor absorbs excess heat in the middle of hot days and then releases it during the night, moderating conditions as the sun circles the earth. This is why deserts have such huge temperature swings in the course of a single day – there's not enough water in the atmosphere there to act as the heat sink.

On top of that, is the fact that water, again nearly uniquely among all liquids, expands just before it turns from a liquid to a solid. This is important, not just so that your ice cubes float in your soda pop, but also so that the oceans, rivers and lakes stay mostly liquid, even in the coldest of winters.

You see, if water contracted as it cooled as most compounds do, the coldest water would sink to the bottom of any body of water and settle there until it froze solid. Over time, the ice at the bottom of all oceans, lakes and rivers would thicken until only the top few inches would melt in warm weather. We would be left with only a very little water in free form to be used by living creatures – in effect no life could survive. All of this is due to the "hydrogen bonds" that hold water molecules together.

Coincidence? Or design? Did all of this happen by chance? Or is there a God?

The strength of the pull of gravity is another anthropic factor that is so fine tuned, it speaks of the existence of an intelligent Creator. If the power of the pull of one massive body on another was either stronger or weaker than it is – by even a small fraction of a percentage point, the universe would either collapse into itself by the crushing pull of the weight of the stars, or it would fly apart in every direction from the momentum of the expanding universe. Either way, we would not exist.

This fine tuned factor is another example of an anthropic principle – the universe seems to have many very finely tuned factors, made 'just so' to enable the existence of life.

The distance of the earth from the sun is yet another example. As you know, the earth orbits around the sun once every year at a distance that is very precisely balanced. At an average distance from the earth of 149.6 million kilometers, the sun's energy, light, and gravitational pull are all exactly 'right' to support life without:

- Boiling away the oceans
- Scorching plant life
- Sucking the earth into a fatal spin into the surface of the sun
- Triggering an unending ice age
- Swinging tides that flood the ground for miles inland

- Pulling the tectonic plates into perpetual 'earth tides' that would cause catastrophic earth quakes
- Blasting the ionosphere away, leaving the earth unprotected from solar radiation

This is no coincidence. Change any of these factors by a percentage point, and you have either a smoldering cinder or an ice block for a planet. Not only that, but if the orbit of the earth was just a bit ovoid, rather than nearly a perfect circle, the same issues would arise. Coincidence? Or design?

What is more, the statistical likelihood of these factors just happening by chance in a random universe, is impossibly remote. Even with the 14 billion years that secular science says have elapsed since the big bang, these anthropic attributes, and many more like them, could not have occurred without some power directing them.

Don Goldstein, wrote in his book, "If I were to drop 5 pennies from the door of a jet flying at 300 miles per hour, from a height of 32,000 feet, what would be the odds of them landing in five perfect lines of 10 each? You would never believe it happened. Yet some people still believe, and ask us to believe as well, that highly complex organisms 'fell into place' on their own."

There are more examples and statistics concerning this topic, but for now let us move into another line of reasoning. For more evidentiary proof of the existence of God, let us explore the internal and external evidence of the Bible itself, and see what this document brings to the debate.

It seems odd that we offer the Bible as proof of itself, but this book is unique, and so internally precise, that it serves as a form of proof of itself. George Otis, in his book "Millennium Man" says that the Bible is 'self authenticating'. Let me explain. The Bible, beyond being just an eyewitness account of events that testify of the existence of God, is such an amazing book that it could not possibly have been written by mere humans without some outside help.

Look at some of the intrinsic factors that make the Bible a unique book in all of history, and among all of the written words placed on paper.

Prophecies that have been fulfilled make up one of the most interesting intrinsic proofs of the existence of God. The Bible contains hundreds of predictions of amazing breadth and specificity, some of which were given hundreds of years before their fulfillment. We will explore three of them here.

In about the year 700 B.C., a man named Isaiah, a well known prophet in ancient Israel, wrote about a King named Cyrus. This king wasn't even born until 150 years later, when he rose to power and became the ruler of the nation of Persia. At the time of the writing of Isaiah's prophecy, Israel still was an independent nation unbothered by Persia. In fact, Israel wasn't take over by the Persians until about 600 B.C.

When Cyrus came across this written prophecy in about 550 B.C., he was so astonished and impressed by the prophecy that named him personally that he willingly fulfilled the rest of the prophecy by releasing the Jews to return to their native land and rebuild their capitol city and the temple. Following is an outline of the events in those days.

- Isaiah wrote his prophecy about King Cyrus in 700 B.C.
- Cyrus took the kingdom of Media from his father-in-law, welding the Median and Persian Empires into one. This

established the Medo-Persian Empire in 550BC, 150 years after Isaiah wrote his prophecy
- This empire lasted about 200 years
- In 539, Cyrus's general captured the great city, Babylon, without a fight
    o Diverted the river/moat, and seized the city quietly
    o Some residents didn't even know they had been conquered for 3 days
    o This action deposed Belshazzar, the king of Babylon
    o 12 years later Daniel showed Cyrus the scroll of Isaiah that had been written 150 years before he had been born
    o Isaiah 44:27,28, 45:1-5 and Ezra each refer to these prophecies in the Old Testament
- Cyrus's response is recorded in Ezra 1:1-4
    o He was very impressed by the prophecy when Ezra brought the ancient text to his attention
    o He frees the entire group of Jewish captives
    o He returned the treasure of golden vessels and temple implements that had been plundered and misused by Babylon
    o He gave the returning Jews financial incentives – actually paid them to return to the homeland
    o He allowed and funded and protected the rebuilding of the temple

Who but an outside, all-knowing intelligence could have predicted such a strange sequence of events a century and a half before it happened?

Next, let's look at the first ten names in the genealogy of the first humans on the planet. This is a list of names that many of you will find familiar – and other than their unusual-sounding syllables, don't seem to mean much to us.

- Adam
- Seth
- Enosh
- Kenan
- Mahalalel
- Jared
- Enoch
- Methuselah
- Lamech
- Noah

You probably think nothing special about this list of old fashioned names.

But let's take a look at the meaning of each of these names:

- Adam - Man
- Seth - Appointed
- Enosh - Mortal
- Kenan - Sorrow (but)
- Mahalel - The Blessed God
- Jared - Shall come down
- Enoch - Teaching (that)
- Methuselah - His death shall bring
- Lamech - The despairing
- Noah - Comfort and rest

Again, you could look at those meanings and yawn. They are simply words in a list. Some of the meanings of those names are also unusual – who would name their child "The Despairing", or "Sorrow"? But when you place them in order of their history, and in sentence form, read it and then tell me you yawn!

Man (is) appointed mortal sorrow, but the Blessed God shall come down teaching (that) His (own) death shall bring the despairing - comfort and rest.

Is it possible that people, 4000 years before Jesus was born, and over the course of about 1000 years, would have named their sons in such a way as to spell out the message of the gospel? Or, as some would argue, and just as puzzling, is it plausible that this message could have been faked by the Jewish rabbi's who hated Jesus, and who lied and murdered to cover up this very message?

Or is it more likely that a loving God moved in the hearts of men in such a way as to ensure that His message of hope and love was recorded in the written record of His interaction with mankind? Which takes more faith to believe? Coincidence? Conspiracy? Or a concerned Creator?

Our third example of prophecies that just might lead an objective reader to consider the existence of God cover the birth and life and death of Jesus. There are at least 300 such prophecies recorded in the Old Testament. Following is a list of just 24 of them.

- He would be born in the city of Bethlehem – Micah 5:2
- He would be born of a virgin – Isa. 7:14
- His lineage would be of the line of Abraham – Gen. 22:18
- Descended from Isaac - Gen. 21:12
- Descended from Jacob – Numbers 24:17
- Of the house of Judah, Jesse, and David
- King Herod would kill children – Jer. 31:15
- He would be a prophet – Deut. 18:18
- A priest – Ps. 110:4
- A judge – Isa. 33:22
- And a King – Ps. 2:6
- He would be preceded by a messenger – Is. 40:3
- He would enter Jerusalem on donkey – Zech. 9:9
- He would be resurrected – Ps. 16:10

- Betrayed by friend – Ps. 41:9
- For 30 pieces of silver – Zech. 11:12
- His hands and feet would be pierced – Ps. 22:16
- He would be smitten and spit upon – Isa. 50:6
- Bruised – Isa. 53:5
- Crucified with thieves – Isa. 53:12
- His garments would be torn, and lots cast for them – Ps. 22:18
- Not one broken bone – Ps. 34:20
- His side would be pierced – Zech. 12:10
- He would be buried in a rich man's tomb – Isa. 53:9

That is a list of 24 prophecies – pretty random descriptions of a man who would be born centuries later - out of about 300 similarly random prophecies. The odds of just 8 of them coming true *by pure chance* has been calculated to be 1 in 10 quadrillion (10 to the 17th)! This is an inconceivable number. Yet it gets even more incredible. The odds of 48 of them coming true by chance? – 1 in 10 to the 157th power.

Let's consider what it might take to have these events happen by chance in a world with no oversight or control by God. Even if the universe is as ancient as evolutionists believe, there would still be only 9 x 10 to the 16th seconds in the entire existence of the universe since the big bang. If there was a trial of options for these events every single second of every year of every millennia - there would still be 10 the 90th **too few trials** for just 48 of these predictions to come true.

In other words, we would have to have 10 to the 90th entire universes, each one trying a different option once every second to have one chance of these events happening all on their own!

Mathematicians and Scientists would all consider such an event happening by chance - Impossible!

The Bible is a message written outside of our universe, by an extraterrestrial intelligence, and sent to us to tell us about the reality of the fact that there is more to life than what meets our eyes.

This unique book presents one consistent central theme, even though it was written by 40 different authors from many different walks of life, over the course of 1500 years, from three different continents, in three different languages. Yet the Bible brings its one overarching story of God's love for people. This written record of God's interaction with mankind has survived through millennia, in spite of both human and Satanic efforts to eliminate it from circulation.

The Bible has never been proven wrong in archeological explorations. In every area of ancient study, from health care to physics, to locations of ruins, to culture and names of individuals, the Bible stands as an amazingly accurate repository of ancient records.

The Bible has been found to record scientifically correct descriptions of animal life, physical properties in chemistry and the cosmos, millennia before such data could be found or measured by scientific means. Details of cosmology, astronomy, the physics of light, gravity, and mathematics, not to mention human nature, psychology, medicine, and history are all described in the Bible long before science figured them out. (For more data on evidence that points toward the conclusion that there is a God, study the book, Evidence That Demands a Verdict by Josh McDowell, as well as studies by Charles Missler at KoinoniaHouse.org.)

And what of simple logic? If you were walking along a path beside a stream, and came across a wristwatch, and found the watch to be running and set at the correct time, what would you conclude? That you had stumbled upon an amazing coincidence of water, mixing sand, moss and dirt together in such a way as to form, by trial and error, this amazing artifact? Or would you conclude that an engineer had planned, and worked with skilled artisans who constructed this intricate machine after careful, meticulous work?

Seeing a beautiful painting, would you not conclude that there must be a talented and experienced painter? Walking through a lovely building, wouldn't your mind immediately know that there was an intelligent and skillful architect and a builder?

These discussions and points of data form a solid evidentiary case proving the existence of God. But let's press the issue, and go on to discuss the second half of our question.

Does God interact with humanity on this planet? Again, the evidence points to 'yes'. And there is too much evidence to ignore, unless you have already made up your mind on the matter. There are two points that prove to the objective mind that God does care. First, the existence of the Bible. If God went through all He has to get the Bible written, and to preserve it through the ages, He must care. Second, is the evidence of God intervening in the events of history (at creation and at the life of Christ, for two examples out of many). Every time we see God acting in history we get a glimpse of His concern for humanity. We will discuss these God encounters in more detail later in this book.

If your world view is already set, and you have decided that there is no God, then you filter, consciously or unconsciously, all data and all evidence – discarding evidence that contradicts your preconception, and you credit only the evidence that bolsters those preconceptions.

Is there a God? It is extremely difficult to conclude otherwise without ignoring all of that data. Yet people do come to that conclusion, just the same. Part of the problem is that we humans come to conclusions based on emotions more than on logic. Our hearts are more convincing and more convinced than our brains. That is why people will often do things that they know full well will destroy their lives. We make decisions based on information seared into our hearts by traumatic events, painful encounters, and emotional events. And once those emotions are burned in, they are tougher to remove or change than a welded joint in steel.

In light of the evidence that supports the existence of God, it is foolish to ignore that evidence and say that there is no God. One of the reasons people decide that there is no God is that living with a world view in which there is a God brings a level of responsibility to live up to a higher standard. "Only the Christian worldview provides the necessary preconditions for the intelligibility of human experience. That is, only the Christian view of God, creation, providence, revelation, and human nature can make sense of the world in which we live." (Brian Fenimore)

If there is no God, or if He does not interact with us, then our actions make little or no difference to our own lives or to the course of history. If there is a God, then what we do matters. Our actions will impact not only ourselves, but others, and will have an even longer term impact than our own lives. We are answerable for what we do to a court higher than our own fallible judgment. We are answerable to God.

In effect, if there is no God, we can relax and do just what we want. If there is a God, then we have to behave. Subconsciously, some decide to disbelieve in God so that they can live a life without that higher level of accountability.

So, if our world view is an emotional, even subconscious decision, why do we even discuss this question? What is the sense in giving data points? Why bother sharing mere information when decisions are so strongly emblazoned deep in our hearts? Because truth combined with God's moving in our hearts can correct even the strongest held misconceptions. Particularly truth in the form of His written word. So feed your heart truth. Look for places where you hold to a lie, and trust God to transform that stronghold of lies into a fertile plot of truth.

Sticky question number one – Is there a God? Yes. Does He interact with us? Yes.

Chapter Two – Who is God? And what is He like?

Once we have come to the conclusion that there is a God, we may start to wonder who He is. And this is a healthy path for each of us to travel, because if God does exist, and if He is involved with the human experience, then we would be wise to know how to interact with Him.

A good place to start this quest would be to look at how He has revealed Himself to mankind. There are two ways He has done this:

1) He has actually stepped into time and interacted with men at specific, recorded times in history.
2) He has sent a detailed communiqué to mankind in the form of a written message called the Bible.

Of the first method of revealing Himself to mankind, there are 6 major interventions in which He has stepped into the flow of time to make clearly noticeable, widely recognized changes in the course of history. And then there are numerous times when He has 'stuck a finger' into the flow of more localized events in the form of miracles.

The six major events include:

1) Creation
2) A curse placed on the earth in response to man's initial sin
3) A major judgment in the form of a worldwide flood
4) A major division in the nations in which languages were introduced in order to separate the various people groups

5) Jesus' birth as described in the Bible
6) Jesus' resurrection from the dead

The "minor" interventions include the many miracles recorded in the Bible, as well as innumerable other miracles that have happened in history, both ancient and modern.

But interventions of God (miracles), whether major or minor, are only believable if A) your world view allows for the existence of a God who interacts with humanity, and B) you accept the fact that the history of the universe is not a "steady state". <*The belief in a steady state universe means that all the processes we see happening now (the speed of light, the decay of radioactive atoms, the rate of erosion, the frequency of meteors and other debris in outer space, etc.) happen at the same rate that they have always happened since the universe began.*> If your world view disallows these two underlying factors, then you are forced to interpret data in such a way as to explain everything as being a result of natural causes, and to exclude data that forces you to accept those two factors.

Once you accept the fact that there is a God who is powerful enough and knowledgeable enough to create the universe, it is easy to see that He might, at times, find it possible and important to touch events in such a way as to impart knowledge of Himself to the people He created. And, indeed, for an all-powerful God, a major intervention, such as Creation, would be no harder for Him than a minor intervention, such as healing a blind man.

It is interesting to note that each of His interventions reveals something of God's nature and character.

Creation tells us much about His power, His creativity, His eye for detail, His organized mind (so much so that people with an atheist world view could look at the myriad species He created, see the organization inherent in them, and conclude that they evolved step by step), and His emotional makeup in creating man and woman in such a way as to express His desire to fellowship with other free will beings.

His response to man's first sin reveals His holiness, and His desire to have humans live up to a standard of holiness. It also exposes the beginning of His plan to bring man back to full fellowship with Him.

The flood shows the reality of man's free will, and the lengths to which God goes in His desire to bring us back to where we belong – in close relationship with God.

The division of tribes and nations at Babel tells us of His plan for man to look to Him for fulfillment and not merely to self-effort and human achievement.

The intricate events leading up to and surrounding the birth of Jesus shows the precision of His foreknowledge, and the depths to which He goes in His determination to honor His promises and His word.

Jesus' victory over death itself tells of God's unstoppable power and extravagant love.

And of the thousands of 'minor' miracles in which He has shifted physical law? These divine interventions are gifted to us for various reasons. They often express His love for us in rescuing mere people from hopeless situations. They sometimes reveal His holiness as He steps in to stop evil from gaining victory. And they always show the reality of His existence – emboldening believers, converting doubters, testifying to the authority of His spokespersons.

And what of His written word? This amazing book – though the word 'book' lacks the power to define the amazing content of what He has done, and what He has revealed in this miraculous tome. Its internal consistency, historical and scientific accuracy, prophetic infallibility, poetic and romantic richness, and complete perfection in its content prove its extraterrestrial origin. No other book in history has faced such opposition and such determined resistance and, not only survived, but spread across so many natural, language, national and continental barriers.

And the detail and supernatural origin of His word reveals His intelligence, and the lengths to which He is willing to go in order to draw us to Himself.

Some have commented on how the Bible seems to describe God differently in the Old Testament compared to the New. And, indeed, there seems to be a tendency for Him to be described as more angry, distant and judgmental in the Old Testament, and more loving, forgiving and forbearing in the New. How can this be resolved? It has been argued that these various descriptions are contradictions within the Word. So, just how is God different from the Old Testament to the New Testament?

As an analogy, ask a child to describe their father – the child will answer differently at different times, not because the father has changed but because the infant's interactions and understanding have evolved with his aging and experience. In the same way, God's interactions with mankind have varied over time as various situations required. He has progressively revealed more of Himself to us over the centuries, gradually giving us a more complete picture of who He is.

So, gradually, as we read through His word, we learn that He is a complex being, having many facets to His personality. Of the Bible's full content we cannot hope to adequately delve in this short chapter. But let us dip our toes into what it reveals to us of God's nature. His word reveals that He is at the same time both holy and loving, powerful and caring, fair and yet has 'favorites' in light of His eternal plans. He is forgiving and just, merciful and jealous. He is creative, with an eye for intricate detail, organized in His engineering, and yet lays plans with patience, and with a long view of the big picture.

In its stories and history are revealed numerous names and character traits of its Author. In my years of reading the Bible, and reading books written about the Bible, I have collected a list of these names and traits. This list is surely not exhaustive, but I share it here.

Eternal One, never changing, perfect, caring

Creator, Sustainer – powerful, an eye for detail, artistic, Genius

Imagination, full of grace, constant, infinite

Savior – righteous, holy, Rock of Salvation, Redeemer

Fortress, hope, perfectly just, merciful, Deliverer

Completely forgiving, powerful, Jealous

King – glory, honor, power, majesty, Defender

Father – need-meeter, wise, loving, perfect, my help

Protector, faithful, lover of my soul, True

Lord – leader, good Master, wise, Sun and Shield, condescending

Shepherd – protector, Lamb that was slain, Provider

Lion of Judah, - my strength, my firm strength

Lord of Hosts – Strong Tower, Cornerstone, Fountain of Living Water

Foundation, Shelter, The Root, The True Vine, Bright and morning star

Almighty God, I AM, Promise Keeper, Abba, Descendant of David

Friend – understanding, companion, faithful, Rock

Compassionate, Comforter, My Peace, Healer, Holy Spirit

Son of Righteousness, Resurrection, our Strength

Wonderful, Beautiful, Counselor, Mighty God

All knowing, Ever Present, Omnipotent, The One Who Sees Me

Eternal, Infinite, Transcendent, Jesus! Consuming Fire, First-born of the dead

Abiding, Indwelling, Immanuel, God with Us, Messiah, Lifter of my head

Priest, The Way, The Truth, The Life, Jesus Christ, Faithful witness

Prince, Captain, Warrior Who Saves, Worthy of my offering

Man of Sorrows, Worthy, Source of my Joy, Ruler of the kings of the Earth

King of Kings, Lord of Lords, My portion, The Pearl of Great Price

The Word of Life, Living Water, Bread of Life, The Prize

Life itself, Anointed One, Rose of Sharon, Living Word, The Source of creation

His name is Love, Prince of Peace, Way Maker, The Amen, The Faithful, True Witness

Light, Alpha, Omega, Holy, Holy, Holy! Breath of Life

Yeshua Meshiak   Adonai   Yahwe

El Shadai – Almighty God

10 "Compound Names" –

Jehovah Jireh – Provider, Redeemer

Jehovah Rapha – Healer

Jehovah Nissi – My Victory

Jehova Elyon – The Lord Most High

Jehovah Shalom – My Peace

Jehova Sabaoth – Lord of Hosts

Jehovah Raah – Shepherd

Jehovah Tsedeq – My Righteousness

Jehovah Shamah - Present with me

Jehovah Maqadash – My Sanctification

There is value in reading about and contemplating who God is. Understanding who the Creator is and what He is like can shed deeper understanding on the events that surround us. And knowing Him better allows us to trust Him more fully as we follow His leading and receive His promises. His names help fill out a clearer picture of who He is, just as our own various titles in life reveal more of our image to people around us. The titles of father, husband, brother, board member, musician, and author each tell you a bit more about me. In the same way, each of God's titles, names and character traits reveal more of who He is, and how He can be expected to respond in different circumstances.

There is also value in developing your own list. As you seek Him, and as you encounter the Author in His word and in His creation He will unveil His names and character to you. These titles and traits will impact you in deeper, stronger ways.

One other aspect of God's being should be addressed here. The Bible never mentions the word "Trinity", but it is clear that the Bible does describe God's nature in such a way that the word describes His three-part nature quite accurately.

Various verses in the word of God tell us that there are differences between God the Father, God the Son (also known as Jesus Christ), and the Holy Spirit. Each of the three are described in various verses as having been present and playing a role in creation, in the salvation of people, and in the ongoing life of Christians. Furthermore, Jesus tells us that He was abandoned by the Father at His crucifixion, the Spirit joins with the Son at His baptism, and the Son prays to the Father just before His betrayal.

We, too, are instructed to pray to the Father, in the name of the Son, and with the assistance and leading of the Holy Spirit. Much is purchased for us by the actions and sacrifices of the Son, revealed to us by the Spirit, and made available by the power of the Father. Jesus is called the Living Word of the Father. Jesus returned to the side of the Father in heaven at the moment of His resurrection, and sent the Holy Spirit to baptize and fill us. His word promises us that everything we need for both life and godliness is available through the true knowledge of the Father.

And what of God's interaction in the stream of time? He exists outside time, yet dips into it on occasion, changing events for His own purposes. Keep in mind that time is a physical dimension, just like height, length and width. And just as we can move through altitude, length and breadth, God can move through time. While we can manipulate the three dimensions we know of as distances, we are stuck moving along with the currents of time without the ability to move against that current.

But God can! He can step into and out of the passage of time at will, just as easily as we can step forward or to the side on an open floor. Because of this, He can both know what will happen years ahead of time, and still leave us with the freedom to make decisions. We can, at any time, say yes or no to going to the store, we can make decisions, both insignificant and profound, and He knows all along what will happen.

This is a paradox, a mystery too great to comprehend, until we begin to understand His ability to move through time. God is not a passive passenger in the passing of time as we are. He transcends time.

Before we leave the topic of 'who is God?' it might be interesting to briefly discuss the idea of God's glory. Just what is His glory? One definition that brings some practical focus to the question is "His Character". If that is true, then we can see and appreciate His glory more and more as we learn of and understand the various aspects of His character. This directs us again to His word, and to the list of names and character traits, and urges us to learn to know Him more intimately.

Who is God? What is He like? We may scratch the surface of the answers to this question in a book like this, and we may spend the rest of our lives – no, the rest of eternity – exploring ever deeper levels of the never-changing, eternally infinite God. One of my favorite names for our God is "The Prize". As such, He is truly worthy of a lifelong search for more of Him.

Chapter Three – The hand is quicker than the eye!

Are there such things as miracles?

Going back to our first foundational questions, if we have concluded that God exists, and that He does interact with humankind, then it is a simple thing to see how His interaction with the physical plane would take the form of what we see as miraculous events. (Can you see how your worldview is so pivotal to answering the rest of these questions? If you haven't settled that first question in your mind, go back to first chapter and review the logic and arguments, and reach a conclusion, for the rest of this book will be of little benefit to you until you can deeply believe that there is, indeed, a God who interacts with us.

It is interesting to note how people react to the idea of miracles. It is common for people to be able to allow that certain miracles may happen, yet hesitate at, or reject the possibility of others. Some will say that, certainly God can heal a person of a disease, but no way could Jesus be born of a virgin. Sure, He could make a fishing trip by his disciples become suddenly productive, but He could never split a sea and then drown a pursuing army in the returning flood. Sure, He could multiply food to feed a bunch of people. But flood the whole earth, saving only eight people in a homemade ship? No way.

In my mind, this makes no sense. If God is God, if He has power, if He can step into history and change some physical laws, then He can step in and change any physical law He chooses. One miraculous event is no harder than any other to Him who exists outside of time and space. He who made the universe with all its physical laws, can suspend them at times for reasons of His own.

One way to visualize His miraculous interaction with us is to envision, if you can, a two dimensional person living in a two dimensional world. This person would look to us like a stick figure drawn on a piece of paper. His entire life would take place on this plane, and his encounters with other stick people would consist of touching within those two dimensions. In fact, it would be difficult for these two-dimensional people to contemplate anything beyond those two dimensions.

If, however, you and I (as three dimensional people) were to try to communicate with those 2D people, it could only happen as we somehow intersected their two dimensions. Further, their awareness of our interaction with them could only be perceived as a 2D interaction within their plane of existence. As our three dimensions came in contact with, intersected, and passed through their 2 dimensions, they would notice it only as another two dimensional entity, and they would have no way of knowing that there was more to us than the two dimensions they encountered. To them, our interaction with them would be an odd event, far out of the ordinary, and explainable only as a temporary suspension of the laws of their 2D world – a miracle to them. Our 3D effort to communicate with them in their 2D world would be analogous to God interacting in our world.

Science has, in the last decades, and through the efforts of advanced mathematics and physics, found that, while we are aware of 4 dimensions in our daily lives, there are actually ten dimensions in our universe! So if there is a God, and if He created the universe, and if He interacts with us, then His 10D self is interacting with us in our 4D world. And when that happens, it appears to us as unusual, supernatural suspensions of physical law – miracles.

A ten dimensional being would have no more trouble interacting in our four dimensional world than we have in interacting with a piece of paper.

Miracles of any sort are no trouble to such a being. The only remaining question is, "Why do miracles happen so rarely?" When we see a world so full of need, why does God so rarely step in to change things for the better? I can think of at least three reasons for the infrequency of miracles.

One reason has to do with the free will that God knit into the makeup of humans. Our ability to choose whether or not to walk with God, to accept His will for our lives or not, is an essential part of what makes us humans. If God were only interested in people obeying Him, He could have made us without the option of disobeying. While this would have led to a world without danger and sin, it would also have resulted in a world without beauty, love and relationship. Only with the freedom to choose can man freely create, obey and enjoy relationship.

Interestingly, a second factor that seems to limit the frequency of miracles has to do with what makes a game a game. We could use any game as the basis of our discussion here, but let's use baseball for our example. Baseball has a list of rules that each team, each player, each coach, and most importantly, each umpire agrees to follow. The rules make the game understandable, and define the game. As soon as players begin ignoring rules, the game degenerates into a free-for-all in which the strongest impose arbitrary rules on the weakest – and there is no longer any game.

The same is true of the way the universe runs. God made the 'game' of life with certain rules. Gravity, momentum, and the speed of light are rules, or laws, that make the game work in physics. Human health also has rules that make it work. Rules about nutrition, exercise, proper sleep and cleanliness make life possible and understandable.

Conceivably, God could change the rules at any time. He could suspend the law of gravity, or decide that we can eat all the sugar we want without negative consequences. However, as soon as He started ignoring the rules, in the form of miracles, the game would be over. There are no longer any understandable boundaries by which we can plan our lives. So there are limits on how often God can suspend the rules and still have life work. The rules of the game define the game, even for the umpire.

Finally, if God were to step in and change every negative aspect of our existence, there would no longer be any need for us to have or use faith. And God, for some reason, has established His relationship with us with a high level of importance placed on us using our faith in our pursuit of a relationship with Him. If He were to do miracles in every case of need simply because the need existed, there would be no room for believing His Word or His promises, for everything that we take on faith now would be visible and proven. Every promise He makes for our lives would be seen, felt and measured rather than believed by faith in His Word.

So faith is a "leap" into the un-measurable after the end of all of our measuring and seeing and knowing. It is the taking leave from what can be touched, and the landing in the manifestation of the revelation of who God is, and what He wants us to know and trust about Him.

Why does He value faith so highly? I don't know. But it is clear from what He has shown us in His Word, that He does value it more highly than anything else we can do for Him. More highly than sacrificially giving to Him, more highly than our vows to Him, more highly than our service.

Still, there are times when He can, and does, step into the stream of our existence, and change the rules of the game. He has the power. He has the authority. As we learn more of the rules – physical, as well as spiritual, we may better understand how and when He steps into the process in ways that appear miraculous to us time-bound humans.

It may help to understand that the spiritual laws supersede and overrule the physical laws. So it is imperative that we come to understand those spiritual laws as thoroughly as possible. In this way we can cooperate with God as He rules the game.

Within these laws, physical as well a spiritual, we function. It is apparent that He has given us the ultimate rule book, and we can learn the rules as they are spelled out in that book. He has given His spiritual children (Christians) power and authority to use the spiritual laws as we work within His will in caring for and stewarding the resources we hold on this earth and in this life.

At times, as we apply spiritual law, it will seem to those looking on, that we are changing the physical laws – performing miracles. In truth, what is happening is that we are imposing the higher laws of spirit onto the lower laws of physical. Just as the higher law of aerodynamic lift will supersede the lower law of gravity in proper conditions, the higher spiritual law of "By His stripes you are healed" will supersede the lower law of paralysis or blindness or sickness. So people will be healed, we will be given insight and truth and knowledge where we could not have that knowledge without spiritual input from Him.

Unfortunately, many Christians remain unaware of these higher laws. Untaught in the knowledge of these truths, they remain ignorant of the fact that they have this power and authority. So most live lives devoid of miraculous experiences. They are saved, but are living without the spiritual influence they could have.

God has literally stepped into time to act at times in history. As spiritual law is imposed on physical law, miracles certainly do happen. Constrained by the 'rules of the game', miracles don't occur every moment, but they do happen.

Chapter Four –Options in Origins.

Where did we come from?

The question of where we came from has been so beaten up and trodden upon by teachers, politicians and well-meaning pastors that we tend to yawn when the topic comes up. The defenders of the two main theories on origins are so adamant about their pet theory that logic takes a back seat to emotional, territorial defensiveness. Yet the origin of human kind is more than a merely academic question. Where the first humans came from is a key piece of thought process that drives how we each, individually come to conclusions on the value of life, and purpose in life.

This topic is a prime example of how important our world view is, for with a humanistic, mechanistic world view in which our basic view of life is that there is no God, the logical conclusion is that man came into being by merely mechanistic means – evolution from primordial goo. There is no alternative – so even if the steps of evolution make no sense, and though they contradict proven laws of physics, and regardless of the fact that they have little basis in experiment, and absolutely no basis in fact, evolution is the only option open for contemplation. The result is that intelligent minds go to great lengths to explain away the problems with the theory of evolution in order to cling to a theory that protects their preconceptions concerning the non-existence of God.

If, on the other hand, we believe that there is a God who is powerful, intelligent, and full of purpose, then evidence and logic point to the conclusion that life can easily arise as a result of such a God reaching into matter and creating things in an act of artistic creation never seen before or since.

So what does the evidence suggest? As discussed in Chapter One, if there is a God who interacts with our physical world then there is no problem with Him shaping both events and matter in a way that furthers His plans. He could easily exert His will and create three or four-dimensional matter from His 10 dimensional existence.

The biblical record tells us of this very fact – that God spoke and things came into being. That same record has engendered a library full of conflicting opinions on how this could be. One of the greatest conflicts in this topic is the evident contradiction between the apparent age of the universe – estimated by science at well over 16 billion years – and what an evaluation of the first chapter of the Bible would seem to say its age is – about 6 thousand years.

Evidence such as carbon dating techniques, the vast spread of the universe, the current speed of light, the fossil record, and so on would seem to support the age that science claims. But when we look closer at the available data, there is just as much, if not more, evidence that would disprove that multi-billion year age.

Let me list a few of them, and then encourage you to dig in further to find an answer to this conflict.

First there are problems with the carbon dating systems themselves. The data these dating systems provide are far too broad to come to any definitive conclusion concerning precise ages – offering dates that span billions of years. Furthermore, they rely on an assumption that because the nuclei measured for carbon dating degrade slowly and at a steady rate now, they always have. This trust in a "steady state" (the theory that says that the way we see things occur now is how things have always occurred) forms extremely weak links in the chain of reason that leads to an ancient universe conclusion.

In fact, credible evidence exists, and is mounting, that would say that our universe is not in a steady state. Evidence is mounting that seems to imply that key 'constants' that science has come to depend upon are not constants. Recently a solar flare was shown to coincide with a fluctuation in an important nuclear decay 'constant'. Measurements of the speed of light over the course of time in which such measurements have been possible show that the 'constant' speed of light "C", so pivotal in physics equations, is not a constant at all. Measurements of that speed, graphed and extrapolated over time, show a hyperbolic curve that indicates that light moved far, far faster four to six thousand years ago than it does today!

Time itself is now known to be a non-constant, but is instead impacted by other forces of nature such as gravity, acceleration, and speed. So in the beginning, when all matter was tightly packed into an intensely-high gravitational point, time was expanded by an exponential factor of 10 to the 12th power. So at the time of creation one day was the same as 8 billion years! Then, as the universe was formed and spread by the hand of God, gravity diminished dramatically, and time slowed. So day 2 was the same as 4 billion years.

Day three = 2 billion years

Day four = 1 billion years

Day five = ½ billion years

Day six = "only" 250 million years

By the seventh day the universe, and therefore gravity, had spread and time had slowed to only 10,000 times what it is now. By the time of Christ (about 2,000 years ago) a day was only a small multiple of what it is today. And studies over the last few decades show that the speed of light is still slowing, though at a far lower rate of change. These studies are outlined in more detail in Chuck Missler's "Cosmos" writings and CDs.

A variation in the speed of light impacts all of the underpinnings, theories and conclusions of belief in an ancient universe. Suddenly light that traveled from mega-distant galaxies needs, not billions of years to reach us, but only thousands. Radiographic dating techniques no longer indicate a multi-billion year old universe, but a much younger one.

This makes other findings fit more easily into a creation time line as well. The amount of silt in the major river deltas of the world does not allow for an ancient earth. The amount of dust piled up on the surface of the moon does not allow for an immense amount of time during which cosmic radiation and decay of the lunar surface could add up. The salinity of the oceans does not allow for eons of time during which salts and ions have been accumulating. Factors such as these may allow for a multi-millennia old universe, but not a multi-billion year old universe, and no other explanation has been given to account for these measurements.

The amount of free space dust encountered by satellites in orbit around the earth is too great to be encountered in an ancient universe. There should be very little free space dust out there if the universe is ancient, because the stars' gravitational pull sweeps dust out of the vacuum of space at the rate of 100,000 tons each day. If the universe were really multiple billions of years old, there would be no dust left in the near-vacuum of outer space.

Many other measured factors – the pressure behind oil well gushers, the existence of "Radio Halos", the half life of certain radioactive elements, the heat of the core of the earth, and more – could not possibly be the way they are if the earth were as old as the "old earth proponents" hold it out to be.

So the facts that the earth had a beginning, and an age of less than 10,000 years are not contradicted by research findings unless you look at only carefully 'vetted' portions of the evidence.

Next, is the biological evidence found in living systems. There is a physical law called the law of irreducible complexity. It says that a functioning system can be reduced to a certain level of complexity, a specific minimum number of components, and no further, and still remain a functioning system.

A simple example of this is the common mouse trap. The mouse trap we are all familiar with is made up of five components, each of which is necessary, and without any of which it could not function. The parts are:

- a base on which to mount it,
- a spring,
- a trigger,
- a latch, and
- a staple.

If you were to take away any one part of the trap it would have no use. If you were to rely on evolution to come up with a mouse trap, the device would have to come through five distinct assembly steps before it would add any benefit to the survival of the host producing and using the trap. So if the host were to evolve a spring without the other four components, that spring would sit there with no use until all four other parts evolved. Since there is no benefit to the host in having the spring by itself, it would not be passed on to the next generation of hosts to build upon or improve. This example is a simple five component device that a human brain came up with in solving a problem faced by millions of people around the globe.

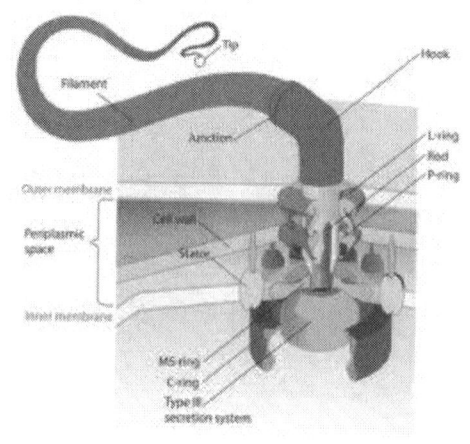

Let's step it up a notch, and look at the mechanisms involved in the flagellum of a simple once-celled organism called a bacterium. This mechanism is a compilation of at least thirteen distinct parts – and again, any of them by itself is a worthless piece of machinery, encumbering the cell without contributing to its survival or procreation. Evolution would have us believe that over time, cells, without the benefit of intelligent, creative, purposeful assistance from outside the cell, came up with all thirteen parts in the right place, in the right order, and all at once, by pure chance. As we will see when we discuss the laws of thermodynamics, this goes against the physical laws which dictate such activities in nature. We will also see, when we discuss mathematical probability, that there is not time enough in all of the universe for such machinations to occur by trial and error.

This is all impossible for even a relatively simple organ in a simple bacterium. Let's move on to something even more complex – the living, functioning eye. The eye requires the simultaneous existence and function of many, many parts, including the eyeball itself, an iris, lens, retina, blood flow, protective mechanisms like the eyelid, tears and tear ducts, eyelashes, aqueous gel, cornea, focusing muscles, directing musculature, nerves of many sorts, and a brain to interpret the collected data. Again, any one of these parts is worthless by itself, and lacking any one of these the whole mechanism is worthless. The laws of evolution itself would teach us that a functioning eye could not come into existence by the forces of unguided chance.

There are many other arguments that array themselves against the theory of evolution. Consider the implications of digital technology and digital information systems. This technology is interesting in this discussion because it is an example of a system that has no purpose or use at all unless all the components of the system are in place at the same time. Those components include:

- A means of gathering information – an input device like a camera or keyboard
- A means of storing the information – a disc or hard drive
- A means of interpreting or sorting the important information – a processing unit
- A means of using the information – a printer or robotic arm

Any one of these pieces of the system by itself, or any two of them without another, are useless. This is a specialized application of the law of irreducible complexity, and it applies to the DNA basis of life on our planet.

Recent study of the makeup of DNA inside cells has revealed that it is actually a digital format of information storage. Wrapped in the code of amino acid chains is a digital instruction book for the building and running of the machinery of life. And just like any digital system, all of the components are present – they must all be present to be of any use at all.

- The information is gathered (presumably by the creator who encoded the DNA, for it had to come from someplace.)
- The information is stored, or coded, in the strands of DNA
- The information is read inside the cells during mitosis by the RNA duplication system
- The information is used at the direction of the DNA and RNA by cellular machinery – the Ribosomes and Golgi apparati

If any one of these incredibly complex apparatuses are missing, the whole cell ceases to function. And, from an evolutionary point of view, all four of these intricate mechanisms must come into existence at once in order for a cell to exist and function. This is impossible. Any one of these mechanisms would take millions of evolutionary generations to come into being, and for all four to happen at once is mathematically inconceivable. Again – impossible.

The laws of thermodynamics are irrefutable laws that define the flow of energy and thermal activity within dynamic systems.

These laws describe the way systems must work in regard to changes that take place over time. These laws apply to our discussion in that they dictate the construction and degeneration of organized systems, such as complicated molecules, cells, and living animals. We will see, as we discuss these laws, that you cannot make or maintain organized systems such as cells or our solar system without an intelligent power acting upon that system.

The **fist law of thermodynamics** tells us how internal energy obeys the principle of conservation of energy, and that mass and energy must be conserved quantities. Basically, in a closed system, you cannot create or destroy mass and energy. You may be able to convert one into the other, but the sum total must be conserved. The first law of thermodynamics states that (without the involvement of an intelligent being more powerful than the universe) there is no matter that can be made from nothing.

The **second law of thermodynamics** demands the irreversibility of active physical processes by stating that the complexity or organization of an isolated macroscopic system never increases. This is called entropy, and it means that all matter and energy must go from organized to disorganized over time unless some intelligent force applies directed energy to organize it again.

This is witnessed by us in many instances of our personal experience – bedrooms become more messy unless someone takes the time to clean them up. Garages will become dirtier and messier unless someone expends the energy to put the tools away and sweep out the leaves and cobwebs. In a car crash, smooth paint gets scraped and dented, and rust will set in unless someone bends the metal straight, sands off the rust, and paints sealant onto it.

In another application of entropy, the second law dictates that heat will always flow from warm to cool – so ice cubes melt, coffee cools, fires burn out, and the universe is winding down from highly organized to eventual heat death – an even, undifferentiated smear of the same temperature. A system on such a trend will have an end. Eventually, the universe will end. And just as importantly, if we track that trend backward, we see something just as profound. Looking at our universe and extrapolating backward through time, the evidence shows that the universe had to have a beginning. Someone had to charge the cosmic battery, wind up the universal spring, prime the big bang.

Sounds like a foolishly simple comment, doesn't it? Yet it is profound in that, when we look at the beginning of an organized system such as the universe, we must ask, "What happened before that?" and, "What made it happen?" These questions, arising from analyzing what we see, lead us back to our sticky questions. There is no escaping them. And the answers lead us, just as inexorably forward to face the importance and impact of ourown decisions and actions.

The **third law of thermodynamics** concerns the state of a system cooled to absolute zero – the lowest temperature possible. You might ask, "Who cares? Who wants to be that cold anyway?" Well, stick with me for another minute here. This law implies that it is impossible to cool a system all the way to exactly absolute zero – a state in which there is absolutely no energy there. Therefore there is always some energy available – a background energy that cannot ever be totally extracted from that system. Even in outer space, empty and cold as it seems, there is a 'hum', or a buzz of energy – (perhaps the subtle energy God uses to sustain His creation, now seen in physics in the existence of the elusive Boson particle?) – holding chaos (the ultimate form of entropy) at bay until He says that it is time for the end of the universe to happen. This application of the third law of thermodynamics may be yet another solid clue as to the existence of God!

These three physical laws beg yet another question. If there are laws in effect, who makes and enforces them? When encountering civil laws, we all understand that laws are made by minds that then enforce them. In the same manner, physical, chemical, and biological laws are another proof that there is an intelligent power behind the veil of our experience. These laws must have an author and an enforcer in order for them to exist and have any meaning.

Now let's turn our attention to the fossil record. Some would argue that the fossilized remains of thousands of species show that simple, small organisms gradually evolved into more complex ones. This is just not true.

While the large number of thousands of species can be grouped into similar looking families, that does not mean that one group led to another. It merely means that we can see similarities in their form and function. There is a critical difference between cause and mere correlation or similarity.

To make an assumption that similarity of form and function result from a common ancestral DNA source through evolution of species is to take an illogical leap into causation that only makes sense to a mind that has already set itself on a world view that says there is no God. With that world view in place, the only other answer for the question of origins is evolution, so the mind that has accepted that preconception goes on to (usually subconsciously) treat as credible only the data that supports that conclusion. However, without that world view, similarities in form and function can just as easily be explained by a common Creator.

With a vast enough variety of species, enough samples will give opportunity to sort them into groups of similar composition. This does not mean one evolved from another, but may indicate that a mind, thinking along a certain track, came up with similar systems while making the large variety of separate species.

As an example of this line of reasoning, consider finding a large deposit of sand. The sand deposit is composed of millions of grains of sand that exist in many colors and shapes. An inquiring mind could examine that sand with a microscope and see the many colors and shapes, and begin to wonder where such a collection of sand granules came from. As his curiosity grew, he might begin cataloging the grains of sand into groups based on the colors and shapes. As he sorted the sand grains he might actually divide them into such groups – reds in one pile, browns in another, cubes piled here, tetrahedrons here. As he continued to sort through the groupings, he might notice that the colors and shapes could be seen to gradually shift from simple to complex, and he could come to the conclusion that all of those complex sands must have come from a single, simply shaped grainover a vast amount of time.

Or on the other hand, if he knew that the sand was man-made, he might come to the conclusion that these various shapes and colors were grouped in his mind, but that they were actually not descended from one another at all. Their seeming flow from one shape to the next is really just a reflection of the fact that there are so many of them, and with so many of them coming from a common intelligent maker, they have some traits in common.

In the same way, the vast collection of biological specimens, all coming from a common Creator could easily have traits in common with one another. A more compelling question is, how could there be so many different species without sharing common traits with one another?

This leads us to the evolutionist's problem of persistent gaps in the fossil record.

> "Darwin's theory relies on minute changes in organisms which slowly accumulate, gradually changing the organism until it eventually becomes a new species. If this is correct, then the fossil record should contain many fossils with forms intermediate between different species. This is not what the fossil record shows."
> Even Darwin saw issues with this problem, as he put it, 'Geology assuredly does not reveal any such finely-graduated organic chain; and this, perhaps, is the most obvious and serious objection which can be urged against the theory.' (*The Origin of Species*)" (Truthinscience.org)

Now, 152 years later, the gaps in the fossil record continue to frustrate evolutionists, and despite their tireless search for fossil record of the missing species between the species, and despite their fervent desire to cling to this theory, the gaps remain. Some have revised the theory to include "punctuated equilibrium" to explain what they feel must have been periods of slow evolution interspersed among periods of evolutionary bursts. But they have yet to explain how or why such mechanisms might occur.

Far from proving that life as we see it now came from single celled ancestors through evolutionary processes, the fossil record is evidence of processes that we still do not understand. It certainly does not disprove the existence of a Creator.

Finally, a close examination of the structure of the first two verses of Genesis allow a bit more time leniency to our suppositions on what the Bible says about origins than is typically taught in Sunday Schools across the Christian world. Most teaching in churches on this topic insist that all of creation took six literal days. From nothing but God himself, to everything we see, plus angels and any other spiritual beings – in 144 hours. Now, again, given a powerful God, I see no reason why He could not do this. But it does not explain some of the factors that indicate that the universe may be older than 6000 years. For example, we can see light that has traveled from stars that are more than 6000 light years away. How can we be seeing light from billions of light years away if that light was only produced a mere few thousand of years ago?

Is there an explanation that allows the first chapter of Genesis to be accurate, and still gives a universe enough time to age as it appears to have – perhaps 6 to 10 thousand years? Look at the first verse of the first chapter of Genesis more carefully. It says, "In the beginning God created the heavens and the earth. And the earth was void and without shape."

Stop! Look at it again – in your Bible it probably says it "the earth **was** void..." but the original language allows for a different translation of that word. And a more fitting translation is probably "the earth **became** void..."

This seems like a minor detail, but that word 'became' opens a whole new possibility of the history of the early earth. Consider the following possible sequence of events.

14 billion years ago God created the earth, the expanse of heaven, and the angels. The Bible does not detail how long that process took, but at some time following that event Satan, initially God's top-ranked angel named Lucifer, got proud and foolish, and decided to revolt against God's rule. God judged Satan and banished him to the earth. While on the earth, Satan 'pitched a fit' and ran amok, ravishing that part of God's creation and rendering it "void and without form".

Then God, in His desire to redeem His creation, re-created the earth in a sequence of events recorded in the next verses and chapters of Genesis. This re-creation could easily have taken place in the six days indicated, if done by a powerful, creative God – the same God encountered over and over in the rest of the written record of God's interaction with our planet.

A connected tangent to this question is the relationship of man to animal. The Bible makes it clear that there is a difference between human nature and animal nature. Man is described as the pinnacle of the creative sequence, not only in complexity, but also in the very makeup of our being. One way to think of this is that animals have a body and soul, but humans have body, soul, and spirit. But what do these words mean?

Obviously it is difficult to draw a line that clearly separates soul and spirit, but there is a difference. It would seem that the soul includes things like personality, emotions and logical thinking, while the spirit is a deeper essence of who we are – including conscience and the ability to communicate with God's Spirit. One potential description of spirit, and the separation between man and animal, is not the ability to think, but the ability to think about what one is thinking – the ability to discern right and wrong.

This is not to minimize the mind of animals, for it is clear that animals can think, and appear to be able to use some level of communication or language, and perhaps even to 'feel' joy, shame, and other feelings. But still, there is a difference. Some theologians suggest that animals, in the presence of human 'managers' can come to have more and more 'spirit' – and exhibit more and more human-like characteristics.

Perhaps the spirit-soul difference should be more accurately envisioned as a spectrum, gradually shifting from one to the other as we speak of emotions, conscience, and other non-body aspects of our being.

The Bible indicates that spirit and soul are both parts of human construction that are eternal, and there is ample biblical witness that our resurrected, perfected bodies will be present in heaven as well.

In Genesis, Adam, and through him, all of humankind, was given a mandate to oversee all of the animal kingdom, as well as the planet itself. It is clear that his descendants have failed in that mandate in many ways, but it still places man over animal in a hierarchy that, if stewarded wisely, would result in a healthy animal kingdom, and a healthy planet.

In looking at the evidence, if it is possible to do so without a bias either for or against the existence of God, it becomes clear that it actually takes a greater leap of faith to believe that the complexities of the universe came into being by random collisions of molecules resulting from a huge explosion billions of years ago, than it does to conclude that God made what we see by His intelligence, wisdom and power.

Chapter Five –All the souls in the universe.

In God's original plan, man was to supervise and care for all the rest of creation. But where do God, angels and other spiritual beings come into this organizational structure? Stories and experiences, myths and anecdotes abound in which God, angels, demons, and even ghosts and aliens are encountered.

Many segments of the timeline of creation, as well as details of the hierarchy of created beings, are only hinged at, or omitted entirely from, the biblical record, and some questions are only indirectly answered, but there are many clues that allow us to consider how all these parts fit together.

Biblically there are only five types of spiritual beings mentioned, including:

- God Himself, in His three persons
- Mankind
- Angels
- Demons
- Nephilim

We have already dealt with the character of God in a previous chapter. People, too, we have described as spiritual beings made unique in several ways. We are "like God". We are spirits made individually and unique, with souls that allow us to interact with each other through the "hardware" of our bodies.

But now let's take a look at the other spiritual beings, and discuss what we can about them.

It is clear that angels existed before man was created. Angels were apparently the first living beings God created. Exactly when that happened is not clear, other than the fact that they were existant prior to the creation of mankind. Their function was to worship God, and to do His bidding.

At some point, however, Satan, who was the finest of the angels and who was initially named Lucifer, got it into his mind that he was better than God. Pride got into his heart, and he revolted against the hierarchy that God had set up. As a result of that rebellion, Satan and a third of the angels were cast out from heaven – banished to earth. There is some debate on when that happened –

- Before or after the six days of creation
- Before man's creation
- After the creation of Adam, but before his sin in the garden of Eden

Most teachers agree that it happened prior to Adam's appearance on the face of the earth. But whenever it was, Satan's banishment to earth has resulted in huge problems for mankind. The Bible describes Satan as "the father of lies", constantly at work seeking those whom he can devour, and committed to his purpose of killing, stealing and destroying. While Satan is a created being, and he does not share godlike qualities such as omnipotence, omniscience, or omnipresence, still he and his demons are dedicated to destroying everything that God wants done on the planet. Key to Satan's plans is his desire to disrupt God's great plan of salvation and redemption, so it is of paramount importance to him to stop people from coming to saving faith. Failing that, he is dedicated to rendering God's faithful followers impotent in their effectiveness as ambassadors for God. To this end Satan develops tactics that include:

- Offering alternative (and false, ineffective) methods of salvation – religions that sound good, but are wrong. This allows literally billions of people throughout history and around the globe to very sincerely believe they are right with God, when they are actually lost.
- Hooking people into addictive lifestyles that offer selfish, sensual, physical or fleshly gratification while rendering their effectiveness for God's plans small and weak.
- Ensnaring people into arguments over theological details that drive wedges of resentment and anger between people who should be brothers in arms. Rather than defending one another against the attacks of the true enemy, and working together to lovingly attract others into the family of God, they end up attacking one another.
- Looking for opportunities to attack, he finds ways to sow seeds of sickness, poverty, confusion, and other debilitating conditions that divert energy and resources from kingdom effectiveness.

Though people tend to fear Satan, and to attribute to him the will and power to face down God almighty in a toe-to-toe fight, he is not as powerful as God is. In fact, the Bible tells us that the authority available to created beings has shifted from one entity to another throughout history. It started with all power being God's, of course. Then, in the Garden of Eden He delegated power to Adam when He told him to care for the garden and name the animals. Next, when man sinned, he surrendered his power to Satan by choosing Satan's lies over God's truth. Two millennia later, God's plan was fulfilled when His Son, Jesus suffered, died and rose, rendering Satan powerless again. Jesus gave that power back to Adam's descendents when He gave His own power and authority to His followers. Since that day, every believer has that delegated authority – the right to speak and act in Jesus' name.

So Satan was stripped of his power when Jesus died and rose from death. The only power Satan now has is what people surrender to him by believing what he says to them rather than what God says. Now, God's words (as written in the Bible) spoken in faith by His reborn children, carry power over all of Satan's plans, schemes and attacks. Brian Fenimore says, "Despite their overthrow, the powers of darkness have not yet conceded their defeat; they continue to contest every inch of their territory. The kingdom of Satan retreats only as the kingdom of God advances." Likewise, Satan's kingdom can only advance as God's children concede ground to him.

Satan's angelic followers, those angels who bought into Satan's lies when he led the rebellion against God, are known as fallen angels, or demons. They were cast out of heaven, and lived on earth during the gap hinted at between Genesis 1, verse one and verse two. They are the beings that rendered God's initial creation "void and without form". They are spiritual beings who can appear in human form and do Satan's bidding. They, like Satan, can impact people through thoughts and temptations, only affecting people physically when people give them access through rejecting God's plan. They never do good, though they may mimic good behavior for a time in an effort to engender trust to further a greater evil.

Angels, like demons, can appear in human form. But that is the only similarity to their fallen, cursed brothers. Angels do God's full bidding. They are good. Always good. They are called ministering spirits. Some of these heavenly beings function full time in surrounding the throne of God, worshipping, singing, acclaiming His holiness and beauty. They serve, first God, and at His bidding, His people. The Word teaches that every living person is assigned a personal angel at birth (or conception). Their job is to protect and otherwise serve their human charge.

There is another type of entity that is described in a few strange encounters in the Old Testament. The biblical name for them is "Nephilim", and they are described as the offspring of fallen angels (in human form) and human females.

The most famous of these beings is Goliath – the giant who was killed by David before he became the king of Israel. Goliath had at least four brothers, and others of these giants are mentioned in other passages – always in conjunction with evil nations that needed to be destroyed by the Israelites as they took possession of the promised land. These giants are described as being about nine to ten feet tall, and as having extraordinary strength. Their existence was part of the reason why the spies who first scouted the holy land were intimidated enough to turn away in fear from taking the land God had promised them. This resulted in 40 long years of wandering in a wasteland, and the loss of an entire generation of people prior to receiving the inheritance God had promised them. Apparently the race of Nephilim were successfully wiped out as a species in those holy land wars.

But what of 'ghosts'? Stories abound of spiritual apparitions found in old buildings or at the scene of intense or unjust deaths. These visitations are usually described as scary, though occasionally as kind, and are attributed to human spirits caught between life on earth and life in the hereafter. But the Bible tells us that humans do not return after death – other than one exception in the case of King Saul encountering the prophet Samuel. So what are these 'ghosts'?

The Bible does not directly address this question, but from what we do know, we can extrapolate that 'ghosts' are really demons appearing to human senses. For reasons of their own, they decide to appear within our four dimensions – again in keeping with their nature – to steal, kill, and destroy lives through deception and confusion.

I suspect we may not fully understand the nature and purposes of 'ghosts' until God deems to tell us in heaven. But certainly I can imagine a demon finding a susceptible human, and communicating to them in an effort to sidetrack their spiritual journey away from "the Way, the Truth, and the Life" that leads to God. Their appearance in human form, seeming to be a person from their past, would be yet another tactic to lead people away from faith in God's plan.

UFO's and alien encounters? Likely the same thing, for the same reason, in a different form. A person with a propensity for science fiction, and a resistance to the Bible's message, would love to explain away a personal God interested in a personal relationship. If intelligent beings exist in outer space, the Bible loses impact in the face of a universe full of beings, some of which are purported to be advanced enough to account for the start of the human race without the need for a Creator God.

So we have five categories of spiritual beings accounted for – God, angels, demons, Nephilim and humans. Ghosts don't make the list because they are really demons masquerading as something else in order to further their evil plans. Animals don't make the list, because even though they have varying levels of intelligence, they lack that mystical ingredient endowed to humans with the "breath of God" at the creation of Adam and Eve.

This is the way God has chosen to organize the universe. This is another important piece of infrastructural knowledge as we build an understanding of the world in which we live.

Chapter Six – Is free will really free?

Do man's choices matter?

This topic is so critical in understanding the impact of the paths we follow during the course of our lives. Recall from our first chapters that evidence supports, and faith confirms, the fact that God is powerful, wise, knows the end from the beginning, and has a plan – a roadmap for every situation and decision that will work out for the best for each person. This is known as His will. So the question now is, "If God has a perfect will in mind, and is powerful, where does human choice come in?"

In fact some would say that God's will is going to be done no matter what individual people do. This belief is included in a doctrine known as Calvinism, named after the founder of this confusing doctrine. Proponents of this interpretation of scripture would argue that man's choices are preordained – not really choices at all, and God will do what He will do no matter what we do. However, this argument, also known as predestination, stands up to neither logic, nor biblical examination. It is a convoluted discussion, so get ready to focus, and sort through the pieces of this argument.

    A. If God's will is going to be done no matter what man decides, then most of the Bible makes no sense. Great portions of Paul's, Jesus' and the Old Testament prophet's writings and instruction become meaningless if man's decisions, and the outcomes of them, are foreordained anyway.

    B. If Predestination controls all of eternity's outcomes, then commands to preach the gospel, to be kind, to deny ourselves, and so on, mean nothing – God will save who He has decided to save regardless of what anyone else does.

C. The passages that Calvinists point to in support of their doctrine, are easily explained with a proper understanding of time and free will.

So what does free will mean? When God created mankind, He endowed each individual with a spirit – an eternal component of our being that allows us to worship God and critically examine what we are thinking – to know right from wrong. He also gave us free will, the ability to choose whether to obey Him or not.

It is apparent that free will is critical to God in His creative expression. Right from His earliest acts of creation, He allowed each sentient being to have this rare gift for themselves. Angels could choose. We know this because some of them chose to disobey. Humans, right from the beginning, could choose. We are told explicitly in the Genesis account that Adam chose to disobey. This decision was called sin. We read of the consequences of this bad choice in the rest of the Bible. And we continue to choose – every moment of every day – either to agree with and follow God, or to disagree and disobey Him.

Still, with all of this gifting of free will to His creatures, He has all along retained His right to govern from the omniscient perspective of His wisdom and expectations. He has never conceded that position.

It is conceivable that God could have made mankind just as He did, but with the sole exception that we have no free will. The result of such a creation might be just like what we would make if we were the creators of humankind – obedient, compliant, safe, and model in their behavior – and these beings would have been robots. Such creatures would be incapable of love. They could obey, but they could not love. I conclude that this is the quality that inspired God to make people – he wanted to love and be loved. But such a quality requires the ability to choose. It requires free will to be able to love.

So this is the key. This is the cornerstone of understanding how God can be powerful, have a perfect will, and still end up with a world in which so many things happen that are obviously not His will.

God, by use of His wisdom and His freedom from the constraints of time, has determined what His best will is for each person in each situation. He has also provided for everything that each of us need for each challenge we face. He has also given us both the power needed to be victorious AND the authority to use that power. So why don't we see people living victorious, abundant, prosperous lives? Why do people step out of His will even when we know what it is? Two reasons.

1) Because we tend to choose what will feel good now rather than to do what will be better for us in the long run. We use our free will and decide to go our own way rather than God's. We choose fleshly, short-term answers rather than looking at how our decisions will impact our lives in long term. And -
2) We fail to appropriate the power, authority and provision God has given us in resisting such temptations.

Combine this failure on our part, with the fact that Satan is earnestly seeking opportunities to take shots at us. He looks for times when we are susceptible to attack. In order to attack, he has to find a way past our defenses, find times when we are outside the protection of God, when we drop our guard, when we fail to use the authority we have been given. Satan and his demons are careful observers of us humans. They develop their strategies from careful study of our posture, what we focus on, what we pay attention to, and what is revealed by our words and actions. From this carefully considered strategy, Satan whispers into our heart, trying to pull us away from God's heart, so that we will fail to appropriate the power, authority and provision God has given us.

So God has His will – perfectly designed to accomplish His purposes. He has a plan that is good for us as individuals, good for His church collectively, that furthers His kingdom, and brings glory to Him. Of course, no one but a perfectly wise and knowledgeable being would be able to orchestrate the lives and decisions of millions of people with the outcome of all the good that He intends from each situation.

Enter free will – even when God lets people know what He wants them to do, even when He makes it clear it's for their own good, even when people find out that doing the wrong thing will harm them and those around them, they still choose to do things outside God's plan. At that point three things happen.

One – things work out in ways that are less than optimal for the people who choose wrongly, for our decisions have consequences. Choose to eat poorly and your health suffers. Choose to use your money on the wrong things and debt becomes a problem. Choose to ignore God's will, and you will live with the consequences of that c hoice.

Two – Along with natural consequences, when we depart from God's plan, Satan has an open door to attack – to do what he does best – steal, kill and destroy lives.

Three – in spite of this, God has promised that all things will work together for good for those who love Him. And as amazing as it is that He can orchestrate a perfect plan in the first place, it is even more amazing that He comes up with a new plan for good (maybe not as good as His first, perfect will would have been, but still good) each time we choose wrong and then repent and seek His path again.

THE TAPESTRY
Viewing a field of tangled lines
Threads of gold woven among the intricate web
Dashes of purity among the dark
Following the glimmering trail
Abruptly cut off
No reason, no cause
Just an end.

Other threads run their course
Dark and subtle, tarnished and frayed
Woven in the tangle, running wild
Simply winding through the mass with no reason
Patternless and random,
 'Til their end

White threads, yellows and greens
Each curving over, under and around
Each start and each end loosely hanging
And I wonder at the arbitrary paths
No explanation for the turns they take

But they, too, meet their end

Looking over the web of these threads
I see confusion in the knots
Tangled mystery devoid of purpose
I shake my head and,
Wondering what the meaning,
Turn away
To what end?

Until arriving at the end of my own thread
I turn back the sheet of tapestry
And see revealed an interwoven wonder
The mesh of knots and hanging threads transformed
Every thread serving the Master's intention,
Will, purpose and form
Art and completion
To His end

There are times when God's will is going to happen no matter what people choose to do. Gravity will continue to operate the way He set it up even if I choose to jump off the top of a building. Water will freeze at the right temperature. Physical laws will continue to run the universe just as planned.

But many, many things that He wants to happen will not happen unless people, with their free will, choose to cooperate with His will. For instance, it is clear from His Word (Matthew 18:14) that it is His will that all humans come to saving faith in Christ Jesus. Yet it is just as clear that not all do. Each day approximately 140,000 people die on earth, and it is estimated that only about 10% of them accept and acknowledge Jesus as their Savior.

It is clear that God takes no pleasure in people dying before their time, yet every day children die from accident, evil intent, or sickness, long before living a long or satisfying life.

Each of us has the choice, every moment of every day, to either follow God's will, or to go our own way. Either option has consequences, and though we may protest, it is usually clear what those consequences are.

Chapter Seven – Who's driving this bus?

Is God really in control?

From our last chapter it can be understood that God has a perfect plan for His creation – His perfect will. It is just as clear that there are times when people opt out of that will. This derails their lives, causing many problems, from illness to placing themselves in dangerous situations, from giving Satan and his demons access to impact their lives in negative ways that would not have happened without the opening, to leading them to unnecessary financial hardships, or missing opportunities in any number of areas of life.

In the long run these negative consequences have even bigger impact. While no one can place the blame for large disasters at the feet of any individual person, still we know that there are huge tragedies that cannot be God's perfect will. Included in this category are things like wars, crime rates, weather damage like hurricanes, tornadoes, earthquakes, and tsunamis, as well as traffic accidents, genetic illnesses, cancer, and more.

These issues are so huge and so apparently out of our control, that we have come to refer to them as "acts of God", and thus to set them off in a category of event that must somehow be His will. Yet if we want to know what His will is in these areas, it would be nice to examine a place where His will is fully accomplished. Thankfully, we have not just one example of this, but two!

Example one – the Garden of Eden. Described in the early chapters of Genesis, we can take a look into what God's creation looked like when His perfect will was being carried out. As described there, prior to Adam's and Eve's sin, we find a picture of paradise, a place where there was no death, no sickness, no cancer, no earthquakes, no storms wreaking death and damage. This was God's perfect will for each of His children. I maintain that it still is God's perfect will for us.

Example two – heaven. While it is possible that no one has ever gone there and returned to tell us about it, we have many descriptions of what heaven is like in the Bible. Among all of these vivid descriptions, there are no descriptions of disasters, tragedies, accidents, or suffering there, either.

The only remaining question is whether or not it is God's will for earth to be like that. In the 4th chapter of Genesis, God gives a short list of things that were going to be different on the planet as direct consequences of Adam's use of his free will to disobey God. Hard work, pain in childbirth, danger, and more were to be humanity's lot in life from that day on – until the day when Jesus defeated Satan, sin, and death. Paul says, in Galatians, that Jesus became a curse in order to do away with the curse that had been placed on mankind since Adam's first sin. But from the day of Christ's resurrection on, God has given man a new option – the option of following His plan again, and living in such a way as to reflect and redeem more and more of His original plan.

How close to paradise we will live on this earth is subject to many things, including damage done by generations of humans disobeying God, Satan's continued attempts to subvert and take advantage of man, and man's inability or unwillingness to use the authority given to him to keep Satan impotent.

Jesus instructed us to pray for God's will to be done on earth as it is in heaven, so it must be a reasonable goal to decrease the frequency of wars, evil happenings, destructive weather, sickness, and accidents. As we learn to take up our authority in Jesus name, and as we learn to receive by faith the things Jesus purchased for us in His final days of life on earth, we will likely still see horrible things happening on the earth. But let us not fall for the trap that Satan sets for us in laying the blame for those destructive events at the feet of God. God is always good, and His will is always for good. Satan is the one who steals, kills and destroys – never our good God.

So what of killer storms and 'natural disasters'? Where do such things originate? In the New Testament, when Jesus and the disciples were crossing the sea and a storm came up, an interesting interaction took place. First, understand that this was no normal storm. It came up suddenly, and it frightened – no, it panicked these seasoned sailors. They thought they were going to die. It is entirely possible that Satan was using nature to try to derail God's plan for the Messiah by killing him in a freak storm at sea. Furthermore, Jesus, upon wakening in the storm, calmly stopped the storm by rebuking it (much like He rebuked the fever in Peter's mother-in-law) and then reprimanded the disciples for their failing to do it for themselves.

This story tells us much about nature, the potential origin of dangerous weather, and the role we can play in it. Certainly storms happen – but these are never the best plan of the God who created beauty and called it good. Do you see the patterns here? Satan uses whatever he can to destroy God's work – even storms. God created weather as a part of the earth's equilibrium. Satan twists it to kill.

And war? Certainly there are times when wars are mandated by human government in an attempt either to seize power by evil men, or to resist evil. But war is never God's highest good.

Accidents also happen, but never as the best will of a loving God for His chosen people. God's best will is for each person to be satisfied with a long, fruitful life. (Psalm 91:16) People die young, not because God "needed another angel in heaven", but because Satan has found a way to attack, kill and destroy another life.

These things, far from being a picture of God's will happening on earth, are resources of Satan, and are the consequences of millennia of people ignoring God's plan.

It bothers me when I hear of people describing a tragedy, not finding anything they can do about it, and concluding, "God is in control." Let me suggest another answer – God is certainly not in control of everything that happens.

"Gasp!"

I know. When I first started thinking about this topic, this statement felt like a rasp running across my mind. "God not in control? But He's all powerful!"

And indeed He is. Yet, as we discussed in the last chapter, He has chosen to design humans (and angels) with free will. You tell me – when a man rapes a teenager and discards her beaten body in a gutter – is God in control of that incident? When a tornado strikes a grade school and leaves broken 3rd graders strewn across the parking lot – is He in control of that storm? When an earthquake drives a tsunami onto the shore of Japan, leaving tens of thousands dead – is God in control?

On a smaller scale – when a man decides to drink himself into a coma – who is in control? When a woman sells her body to gain enough money to buy another hit of mescaline, leaving her baby in a bathtub to die – is that God's will? When a high school student chooses to disregard his need to study, fails a test and loses a scholarship – God's will, or the student's?

It is clear that there are times when God is not in control – not because He is impotent. Not because He does not care. But because He decided to create people who can choose to love Him or not – by their own free will. Part of that decision includes letting people make horrible choices. Part of that deal is letting Satan continue to steal, kill and destroy lives, because to undo free will means turning people capable of love into robots or slaves.

Another specific example of giving God credit (or blame) for more than He should get is when people die. By taking a few verses out of context, some have concluded that no one can die before God calls him home. Is it true that every person who dies, does so exactly when God planned for them to? Is it accurate to conclude of every person who, at an early age, dies from a disease, or from the impact of an accident, or in a war, or some other tragedy, that "it was their time"? That God called them home at that time?

I would argue, no.

A teen driving drunk and too fast when he disobeyed his parents in both driving, speeding and drinking, is far outside the will of God, and outside of God's protection. His accident, in which he and three of his friends die, is not within the will of God. Satan loves such opportunities, but God feels deeply the loss of life, the grief of the parents, the loss of a lifetime of creativity and fruitfulness of every child who dies at a young age.

A 28 year-old mother of two, who dies painfully from cancer is not fulfilling God's promise of a "long and satisfying life." Satan has found a hole in man's cooperation with God's perfect will and has used it for evil.

So what is a "long and satisfying life"? There are varying schools of thought concerning this, but the Bible offers several options – lives were measured in centuries prior to the great flood, 110 years according to Genesis (post-flood, and pre-New Testament), and 70 years according to Psalm 90, verse 10. But nowhere in the word of God does it hint that "it was just their time" is a good measure of a normal lifespan, as in the cases of a 28 year-old mother, a teenaged student, much less an unborn child.

In each of these cases, someone, somewhere has stepped outside of God's will, God's perfect plan, and God's protection, and Satan found a way to attack that life.

It is illogical to think that God would tell us to pray for His will or encourage us to follow His will, if it were impossible for something other than His will to happen. The answer to our current question is that God is in control where He is in control. He has given portions of His plan into the hands of fallible humans to agree with, claim, cooperate with, and carry out if we will, or to reject and walk away from if we so choose.

Chapter Eight – The good. The bad. And the really , really ugly.

Is there really evil in the world?

My initial response to this question is a simple, "Duh!" I mean, take a look around at the world. Listen to the news for just five minutes. Go on line and get inundated with reports of people making decisions that intentionally injure others, leaders leading their subjects to perform mayhem, or people groups cruelly abusing other people groups. Certain Muslim teachings lead to the amputation of hands or breasts from people who break extrapolations of their laws. So-called Christians have murdered Jews for imagined faults. Hindus kill Christians because they have had the audacity to share truth with other Hindus. Any one of these examples will show multiple instances of pure evil being consciously, willfully inflicted on other people.

But even so, people occasionally ask the question. Generally the question is asked in connotation to a less graphic or intense example of evil, rather than in the 'big ones' like war, rape, or genocide. So perhaps a more accurate question might be, 'Is there really an absolute right and wrong?' Or is one man's wrong subjective enough to be another man's right?

Across nearly all cultures, some things are consistently held to be wrong – murder, stealing and rape are examples. Others are just slightly less universally considered wrong – lying, stealing food to survive, exceeding posted speed limits, and cheating on an examination, for instance. And then there are actions that are considered wrong only to a few very conservative people, like watching 'bad' movies, gambling, or gluttony.

The question becomes one of where the line between right and wrong lies. And who draws that line? And is the line the same for everyone?

The Bible is very clear on some of this, and not so clear in other areas. It distinctly declares that it is always wrong to murder – but then teaches that war, in some cases is justified. It says that lying is wrong, yet gives examples of God's people lying, and being rewarded or blessed – if not because of it, then in spite of it. The Bible tells us that sex outside of marriage is always wrong – but tells of Jesus forgiving the prostitute, and letting her go with an admonition to sin no more.

Later in the New Testament, the instruction is given to avoid certain activities when the doer is not convinced it is right to do the activity in question. (Romans 14:23) This leaves a great deal of discretion on the part of one who is seeking answers. A list of sins is a lot easier to follow than the process of listening to our own conscience or the leading of the Holy Spirit.

Suffice it to say that in most cases there is a clear right and a clear wrong. It is only when we reject the objective authority of the Word of God that we find room for relativity in right and wrong. But we are far afield from where our question started us out. Is there really evil in the world?

The Bible teaches that there is evil. And perhaps a useable definition of evil might be – hurtful actions by an individual that are devoid of concern about anybody but self, though we also see evil manifest in this world to the level of intentionally harming others just for the joy of seeing them suffer. And indeed we can see that there are examples of this – obvious ones like a rapist who simply takes for their own satisfaction, or a ruling despot who gathers for himself regardless of the cost of all in his path.

But when discussing the lighter shades of evil, the selfish acts of common people who make bad choices that hurt others, who is to say at what point one has crossed the line between what is just a bad decision and what is truly evil? Certainly not all acts of selfishness are really evil. People who can't think clearly, due to mental incapacity, brain damage, or emotional damage, surely can't be called evil when they do things that are wrong yet not intended as evil. They may not even be able to conceive of the action as wrong.

I would stipulate that even these instances of "innocent wrong" are indirectly, but just as ultimately, the result of evil. Mental incapacities are a long way from God's original good plan – a plan that was derailed by Satan, sin, and centuries of evil eroding away God's good plan to what we see now.

Still, even in cases where a person is incapable of recognizing it, there is a standard of right and wrong. But who is to say what that standard is? It is impossible to expect every person on earth to come up with the same answer of what is right and what is wrong. With all the myriads of ways we are raised and taught, we will all come up with a different standard and moral code if left to our own logic. Remember, much of our decision process is made on an emotional basis, rather than a logical one.

This explains why some say extra-marital sex is okay, and others say it is wrong. Some support abortion as an option, while others declare it murder. Some fight for legalized drug use, while others argue for restriction. Some say it is immoral to use violence even for defense of the helpless, while others declare a different standard.

That is yet another reason why it is so important to recognize the Bible as the Word of God. If anybody has a right to set standards of morality for all of humankind it is the Creator of that life. It might be helpful to look at the Bible as an owner's manual, developed by the designer of the human 'machine'. He knows how life was engineered, and therefore knows how to best use it.

The rules He sets down in the written word are not so much limits on behavior, as directions on how to get the most out of the life He made for us. Included in the owner's manual is a complete list of what is good and what is bad for the organism He designed and built.

If 'evil' is defined as selfish acts at the cost of others, then the Bible spells out and proscribes many, if not all, of its many faces. And evil is, according to the Bible, personified by the fallen archangel, Satan.

Chapter Nine – How could He?!

How can a loving God allow *that* to happen? Natural and manmade disasters.

We hear daily of disasters in the world around us. Earthquakes burying hundreds in rubble. Tsunamis that wash homes, entire cities, and hundreds of defenseless people away in the space of a few terrifying moments. The disease and starvation that follows such disasters in third world countries. Cancer that strikes with seemingly random indifference, destroying thousands of lives every year with awesome, dreadful deliberateness. Storms that appear out of a cloudy sky and rip families, homes, and trailer parks apart, leaving hopeless tears behind. Armies that rage against innocent people groups simply because they have a different tone of skin color, or speak a different language, or worship differently. Rulers who use poison gasses on their own people to solidify their own power.

How can an all powerful God allow these things to happen? In the face of such occurrences, surely God is either weak, and can't change these things, or He doesn't care about people and their pain, and sits idly by while disasters destroy life after life.

For if He is powerful and sees what is going on across this planet that He created, He surely could not sit back and do nothing while children suffer as they do. Certainly you and I would not hesitate to intervene if we could. We would stop the child pornographer. We would take weapons out of the hands of evil men. We would set fire to fields of poppy or coca plantations before it was harvested and turned into life shattering drugs.

We would eradicate cancer cells and viruses that are untreatable by human means. We would DO SOMETHING!

Surely if He is powerful and truly loves the people and things He created, He would be unable to contain His power while He witnessed drug addicted mothers selling their bodies, not to feed their babies, but to feed their habits. You and I would be driven to act before the next child suffered, or the next body was sold, or the next killer storm fell on defenseless heads.

So what is going on? Is He impotent? Or is He apathetic or blind? Is He too busy?

I believe that there is another answer.

God, by His very nature is powerful. He does care. He sees every painful, desperate situation. And He is more than able to handle all the millions of situations that are occurring every moment. But recall how He has made the world. This universe is not a wind-up toy that He set to spinning, and then let loose to run across the cosmos, randomly bumping into 'walls' just to spin off in another direction. Neither is it a pre-programmed robot which He, in His infinite wisdom, set on a carefully, microscopically mapped, preordained mission.

No, this world is an active macrocosm on which He has placed billions of living beings, each of whom has free will to do what He recommends, or to rebel and go their own way. In His wisdom, He has designed this universe to run under the rule of laws that determine how things work. Physical laws, such as gravity, to control the orbits of planets and to keep us safely attached to the surface on which we stand, momentum to keep objects in motion, friction to allow us to move when we need to, nuclear forces to hold atoms together, electrical laws to command the flow of electrons – all of these are intricately orchestrated to keep the universe running smoothly.

In the same way, spiritual laws are in place to guide and control the ongoing functions of life. Spiritual laws include such things as the law of sowing (seeds planted bring a like harvest), the law of jurisdiction (God's gift of spiritual authority can be given to another person on behalf of one who cannot take authority for themselves), the law of spoken words (the spoken word carries power when backed by belief in Truth), and others. These spiritual laws have consequences when they are broken, just as the physical laws do.

In His wisdom, God set these laws in place to provide for an ordered, productive life. The long list of tragedies and disasters that history reveals is credited to man breaking the laws and reaping the consequences of those infractions.

Even "natural" disasters can be traced back to the original sin that mankind committed when Adam and Eve decided to break one of God's first laws. Since that day, the universe has been dying a slow death. The Bible teaches that the earth is groaning in its anticipation of the promised renewal at the end of this age. (Romans 8:22)

In spite of these constant reminders of what happens when God's good laws are broken, most (probably all) of us human beings opt to do what we want before considering what is best. We do what our flesh wants us to do long before considering what God wants us to do. So we continue breaking the laws, setting up the consequences that follow with predictable regularity. It is an amazing part of human nature to see us choosing to do wrong even when we know that the consequences will destroy our lives.

Duane Feldpausch put it this way:

> "Using our free will to choose to follow our own independent path has the result of 'binding' God from protecting or intervening on our behalf. The resulting calamity of separation from Him communicates our desire to be free of His best providence and plan. Rebelling before Him, running from Him, alienating our connection to Him, no longer valuing His best advisements, all have the same effect; the result is an unmistakable separation from His intended future best on our behalf. An evil consequence of the loss of his benevolent protection will always feel like we are in the crosshairs of evil and impending doom."

We have ourselves to blame for this, but Satan also shares in the blame. For he is constantly seeking where and from whom he can steal, destroy, or kill.

But God offers a way out! If we will only take it, He offers promises in His Word – promises and provision already paid for and available. It is up to us to learn of those promises and take hold of them by faith. These promises include:

- Forgiveness for past sins – 1 John 1:9
- Victory over the penalty of sin – Acts 22:16
- Victory over the power of sin to go on controlling us – Galatians 5:1
- Eternity in heaven – Mark 10:17
- Healing for our bodies – 1 Peter 2:24
- Provision for every one of our needs – Philippians 4:19

- A good plan for our lives – Psalm 119:105
- A fruitful, abundant, productive life – John 10:10
- The opportunity to invest our resources in ways that will bear eternal benefit – Proverbs 3:9, Matthew 6:33
- Wondrous works like Jesus did – John 14:12

God has provided everything we need to live a wonderful life, even though we have screwed it up so badly. The question is not so much, 'How can He allow disasters to happen?' as it is, 'Why do we go on ignoring His provision to avoid disasters?'

CHAPTER Ten – Pearly gates, and lakes of fire.

Is there really a heaven and a hell?

This is a difficult question only if you refuse to recognize the Bible as the authority in spiritual matters, because that book states, with no uncertainty, that there is both a heaven and a hell. Without the Bible as the guidebook to things eternal, we have very little data from which to draw conclusions on the subject. We can look for eyewitness accounts, but they are few, and to many, suspect. Those who report near-death, or return-from-death experiences almost always report a warm, bright, overwhelmingly positive experience. This poses a contrast to the biblical report that there are two possible destinations after death, and the location to which most people are going is not a warm and fuzzy place. So how do we resolve this apparent discrepancy?

If we assume that the personal accounts of returning from death are true, and that the person really did die and go to a real afterlife place, we can account for the nearly 100% reporting a vision of a good, comforting place by recognizing what the Bible really teaches about death. The teaching is that people will spend forever in either heaven or hell, but that first they will face God (presumably in paradise, a pleasant place) for their judgment. Thus every person first goes to the warm, bright, overwhelmingly positive place where God presides before being sent to their eternal destiny. If such a person returns to their physical life again at this point in their trauma, they will report their experience up to that point – the time before they were to be consigned to their eternal destiny.

Before we continue with biblical teaching on the matter, what other support do we have for the existence of eternal destinations? Logic does not seem to help us much, other than telling us that our existence is pretty futile and meaningless if life simply ends when the brain stops functioning. Human as well as animal life can be explained away as a mechanistic, simply biological process if you have landed on the "there is no God" side of the world-view question in chapter one.

However, once you allow for a spiritual component to life, you have to wonder what happens to that spiritual component once the biological component is no longer functioning. The spiritual, existing in all of the ten dimensions, and not constrained by time, will go on functioning someplace. Thus, logically, we are left with the need for a heaven, a hell, or someplace else to 'be' after death. Apart from eyewitnesses, it's impossible to know what that place will be.

This leads us back to eyewitnesses of another sort – the ones who recorded their experiences in the Bible. There are several authors recorded in that book who saw portions of heaven and hell – John, in Revelation, Elijah, Jeremiah, and Paul in other books of the Bible. So what does the Bible teach about heaven? And what of hell?

This is a riveting topic, with many glimpses recorded. If you want more in depth discussion of what the Bible teaches on the topic, read Randy Alcorn's book by the title, "Heaven". Here are some highlights of biblical teaching on heaven and hell.

Hell is eternal, and is the destination of Satan, his fallen angelic followers (called demons), and all those who have rejected God's provision for getting into heaven. Hell is indescribably miserable – not a place of partying with friends who have also rejected Christ's payment for their sins, and His offer of free forgiveness to anyone who will receive it. It is described as burning hot, full of unending torment and everlasting pain, complete with intact memory of what life could have been, and the clear recollection of the missed opportunity to go to heaven. Think about a "Mulligan Moment" in your past – one of those moments that you'd give anything to have a 'do-over'. Multiply that by infinity and eternity, and that is a portion of what memories will be available in hell.

Hell was not, however, designed for humans, but for the eternal imprisonment of Satan after he rebelled against God. Humans only go there after rejecting God's offer of reconciliation and forgiveness – in effect choosing to believe Satan's lies rather than God's Truth.

Heaven, on the other hand, is going to be as good as hell is bad. No tears, no pain, no death. According to the Bible's descriptions, heaven promises an eternity of perfect health and unending opportunities to learn of God's goodness and wisdom. Imagine an eternity of learning how to live as He initially intended us to live – walking in unashamed holiness, with unhindered expression of creativity, and exploring and taming the immense expanse and variety of eternity. We will experience all of the very best of what we have now, but without any of the hindrances that darken life on earth now. We will be conscious and aware of who we are and who we are with. Sharing and loving with no hint of shame or selfishness.

The Bible is full of verses that give us glimpses of what life will be like after we 'move in' to our eternal abode. It will be life at its sweetest – forever.

Is there a heaven? A hell? Logic, the Bible, and eye-witnesses all seem to say 'yes'. And this answer brings meaning and purpose to an otherwise senseless existence.

Chapter Eleven – I don't care. Yer outa there!

What happens to people who have never heard? How can a loving God 'send people to hell'?

This is perhaps the most perplexing question I have come across in my search for truth. I am fully convinced of the existence of a personal, good, powerful God who interacts with His creation. There is enough objective evidence for me to have come to the conclusion that the Bible is His specific revelation of at least part of His character, purpose, and story to us humans. I can understand a bit of the impact and importance of our free will in choosing to live out His perfect will or not. But, if the Bible is true, then it is also true that Jesus is THE way to the Father, because it clearly states that truth in John 14, verse 6. And if He is THE way, then other ways don't exist. The other 'paths' to heaven don't work no matter how comforting it might feel to think otherwise.

This narrow-minded doctrine is serious, partly because many people are on the wrong path, and partly because some people have never had the opportunity to hear of THE way. People who live in backwaters, and remote jungles. People who were raised in countries that are dominated by other religions, and whose borders are closed to the Bible. People who were raised by parents who want nothing to do with God or Jesus. People who died as infants – before they were old enough to hear and understand who Jesus is.

This is a huge issue to resolve if we are to believe that God is truly good. For how could a good God allow a person, whom He reputedly loves, to go to and spend eternity in hell? According to the Bible, He sent His only Son, in the ultimate effort to save each of these people, allowing Jesus to die a miserable death in order to rescue them from such a fate. With such an extravagant investment in His effort to rescue people, would He really allow them to go to hell forever?

In my reading and study of God's plan for salvation, I've seen no clear answer to this one. It is apparent from the teachings of the Bible that some (many, in fact) will end up in eternal damnation. Yet we are given hints in His word, clues to what might serve for an answer to this crucial question. Let's look at a few of them, and then I'll go way out on a limb, and give a theory that might allow for some peace of mind on this issue, while staying congruous with biblical truth.

First, it is important to look at the question itself. Most people who bring the question up, start from the perspective of judging God. They ask, "How could He do such a rotten thing to poor, innocent people?" I would suggest that we reframe the question to one that gives God the benefit of the doubt to begin with.

Reframing the question from "How can God send people to hell?" to "Look at the lengths to which God has gone in providing everything necessary to save them, but they opt out," puts the onus for people going to hell where it belongs – on their own rejection of God's freely-offered provision, rather than on a "mean, judgmental" God.

Given the system that God initially set up, including:

- His beneficent will
- His desire to live with and love humans with free will

- The danger of people using that free will to walk away from Him, and
- The consequences that walking away entail

Given all those items as the rules for life, God still has gone to extraordinary lengths to make sure no one has to live for eternity without Him:

- He allowed His own Son to pay the consequences for our transgressions.
- He has supplied us with His specific written instructions on how to take advantage of His kindness.
- He has sent messengers to us with verbal alerts.
- He has written His character in nature all around us.
- He has placed inside each one of us a heart that warns us when we are moving in the wrong direction.
- And He has done all this in the name of love.

He has done everything possible, short of taking our free will away and forcing us to choose the right path. He has done everything short of sending someone back from the dead to warn us – oh, wait, He has done that too! (Luke 16:29-31)

And still people refuse to listen! Still we attempt to outwit Him, using our human reason to back Him into a corner, and paint His caricature as a mean-spirited God who sends innocent people to hell.

No! God is good. He loves each human. He wants each of us to know and love Him in return.

But what of His word? What does it say about some of these issues? Now we get into answers that are less complete, and less absolute. These answers are no longer "carbon fiber" tough, but might be better described as 'sugary' – maybe even cotton candy. There is still a lot of carbon in them, but they are extrapolated – they are a bit 'spun' or drawn out from information that is in the Word. These answers feel pretty good, but are not built on the same solid foundation as the other things we've discussed. So here's the warning – these answers, while they may be drawn from the word, are also a bit of 'how I hope they may work out'. So, with that conditional introduction in place, are you ready? Here we go.

Of the child who is too young to understand God's plan, there is hope. The church has traditionally taught that there is an age of accountability, before which God grants them grace – imparting to them salvation because they know no better. That age is not clearly given, and probably varies depending on the intelligence and understanding of each individual.

That may be a bit of wishful extrapolation, too, however, because there is no clear biblical declaration of such a free pass to young children. There is also a verse in 1 Corinthians chapter 7, verse 14 where He tells us that if even one of the parents of such a child is saved, it imparts salvation to the under-aged child. So that covers some children, but leaves offspring whose parents are both unsaved in an untenable situation.

Of those who live in remote areas of the globe – the first chapters of Romans tells us that all of creation, the stars, the majesty of the mountains, the wonder of the seas – shouts of His existence. Every person on the planet has seen and heard evidence of the creative genius that points toward a Creator.

On top of that, every person is born with an inner compass that points toward 'right'. The conscience in each heart is a truth detector that tells us when we are walking toward truth or away from it. Again, each individual is without excuse.

In each of these cases, the revelation is limited in its ability to tell us of God's plan. Our nurture – the way we were raised, the world view we were taught in our early years – will shade the message. Still, everyone is given some 'light' – the creation, conscience, etc. The fairness of God could be expected to dictate that those who respond to the light they have been given will be given more light.

If this is true, then even the most remote village tucked away near the source of the Amazon will receive more of His truth – a missionary plane will drop a Bible, a rumor will filter through the untraced miles of God's Son dying for them, a dream of God's plan in the deep of a night's sleep – somehow, God will honor the soft heart's desire to know Him

Let's take this a bit further. While I think there are biblical hints that lead me to what we have talked about above, still, there are instances where it is difficult to see how a person might have a fair opportunity to hear of God's plan for salvation through faith in Jesus before they die. Again, a newborn child, a man born and raised in a strict Muslim country, a woman raised in an atheist family in the middle of an atheist country. But God is fair and just. He does say that salvation is by faith in Jesus' death and resurrection. So here is my theory for such situations. The following scenario allows for the one way to heaven, the need for each individual to choose for themselves, and for the justice of God.

While the Bible contains a verse that says, "It is appointed for man once to die, and after this, the judgment," the following scenario still could fall into the time between death and judgment. The argument requires a series of four steps, extrapolated out to one possible conclusion. Follow this chain of thoughts:

1) The Bible teaches us that God exists outside of time – He existed before the creation of the universe. Time is not the same to Him as it is to us. "A day is as a thousand years..." While we, living in our four-dimensional lives, are caught in the flow of time, He is not.

2) According to Ephesians 4:8-10, 1 Peter 4:6, John 20:17, and 1 Peter 3:19-20, when Jesus died on the cross He went to Hades, the resting place of the dead who are waiting for final judgment, to preach to the people there. The Bible does not tell us what He preached to them about. However, what could possibly be more crucial for the Son of God, recently sacrificed for the salvation of mankind, than to give them a chance to choose salvation? What else would He have gone to preach to them about?

    Those souls had lived and died, yet Jesus went to preach to them for three days. Why?

3) When people die in our post-resurrection age, they leave their physical bodies behind – thus they are pure spirit/soul, awaiting the resurrection of the body in the new heaven and new earth.

    In the mean time, while awaiting that time of resurrected bodies, beings composed of pure spirit/soul are no longer restricted to our time continuum – therefore they, too, are outside of time. No longer constrained to the flow of time, they exist – somewhere – (somewhen?).

4) In light of these points, each of which is fairly easily supported in scripture, perhaps when people die and leave the four dimensions that we understand, they go first to that timeless time and place where Jesus preached to the dead. While there, they too hear the gospel and have one last, fair, clear chance to choose.

Granted, this theory is a theological stretch – not clearly supported in the Bible. But it does bring some sense of fairness to the situations of the infant who died too young to understand, the Chinese atheist who never heard the story of the Messiah, the Muslim, steeped in the teachings of Islam – each of them finally hear the Truth, from the mouth of the Teacher Himself, and have one last opportunity to choose – God and salvation, or their own way, and eternity without God. It sounds 'fair', does it not?

Whatever we do know, and whatever questions remain unanswered, this remains true – God is good and just. Every person who lives and dies goes to an eternity and faces the God who is ultimately, completely and eternally loving and impartially just and fair. Ruth Graham, Billy Graham's wife said, in response to this question, that, every person "goes to meet a perfectly just and perfectly loving God."

Actually, such a sense of 'fairness' is necessary only to my limited human understanding. In fact, God is God. He sees much deeper into the matter than we can, and is certainly not blind to the predicament of the unsaved. At the same time, He is not stuck with our limited sense of what is fair, either.

Whatever means He has chosen to resolve this issue, these descriptions of His character are still true, and the eternal destiny of each completely-loved soul will be decided by this

God – not some capricious, angry, unjust God who looks on from afar with a cold heart. This loving God will never have to apologize to one of His creatures for having failed to sufficiently pursue the errant heart, nor for offering too little in His effort to save them from a horrible ultimate destination.

This, then leads us to our next question.

Chapter Twelve – Can't they all be right?

What is the right religion?

Many people today are so 'nice' that they cannot bring themselves to acknowledge that there is actually a wrong religion. Others are so tolerant that they can't come to acknowledge that any sincere person could possibly be wrong. But if 'A' is true, and 'A' proves that 'B' is false, then 'B' cannot also be true. Of course if pressed, most of them would admit that devil worshippers who believe in sacrificing living children to appease Satan are mistaken. They would admit that, no matter how sincere the devil worshipper is, they are wrong, and are probably not doing a good thing – that they are probably not going to end up in heaven.

But according to these good-hearted seekers of fairness, other – 'nice' religions are probably good enough to do the job for their respective followers. As long as a seeker is sincere in following the tenets of their religion, they will probably end up in the right place in the next life. So long as they are good enough, and follow the rules more often than they break them, they'll tip the scales and end up in heaven.

After all, who could ever doubt that someone as 'nice' as Gandhi, for instance, would fall short of heavenly standards of 'good enough'. Those peace-loving priests of Buddha? How could those guys be wrong? They have dedicated their lives to lighting candles, and living in peace and poverty, and quoting their scriptures.

This is an easy, comforting way to believe. It removes the nasty feeling of 'us versus them', the elitism of 'I am right, and they are wrong', the judgmentalism of 'I know the truth, and they don't.' It eliminates the horrible knowledge that millions of people, who just didn't know any better, are going to hell. It is easy, and comfortable, and convenient to think that all roads lead to heaven if you just believe sincerely enough. It is also lazy, illogical, and dangerous to hang the hopes of eternity on such a wishful-thinking sentimentality. It would be nice to be able to believe that all roads lead to heaven – so comfortable to be able to relax about convincing people that they are wrong. I personally wish it were so – but it's not. There really is a right way, and there really are many wrong ways.

There are a number of specific problems with this "all roads lead to heaven" mindset.

First, I see no way to resolve the many outright contradictions between the various religions. In describing the character of God, one religion says that there is only one God, another says that there are several gods, and Hinduism says that there are thousands. The Bible says that God is love, the Koran says He is angry, and Hindu writings describe the gods in as many ways as there are descriptions of personalities. These various, and contradictory descriptions of God can not all be right.

Some would use the analogy of five blind men describing an elephant differently because they all encounter different parts of it. But the analogy fails to mention that they are all wrong in their description, or that some of them outright contradict one another. If God is interested in humans at all, would he not see to it that what we know of Him is accurate?

How about the nature of Jesus? Most religions will agree among themselves that Jesus was a good man, even a prophet. Only the Bible's witnesses speak of Him as more than just a good man or a prophet. Over and over, the Bible tells us that Jesus was actually God – present and participating at the creation, with God before time began, living eternally, ruling over everything, and worthy of worship. Islam says that Jesus was only a prophet, and that He never died on a cross, much less that He rose from the dead. Mormonism teaches that Jesus was a man who became a god by living a good enough life. They can't all be right.

Jesus' own words attest to His claim that He was God, and His own testimony to that effect was what got Him crucified for heresy. So, either He was a liar (having claimed godhead for himself), or He was crazy (for really believing it), or He really was God. Being a good man is not an option, since if He was not God, He was an egomaniac and a liar, leading millions of people down a path paved with hypocrisy and falsehood.

And what do the various religions say about The Ultimate Goal of Life? One says that this life leads to another life as a new or reborn biological being (reincarnation). Another says the goal of life is to become one with the eternal consciousness. Still another says the highest end of this life is to become a God yourself, and when you perfect yourself, start your own universe. Yet another says that the goal of life here is to live forever in heaven. They can't all be right!

And as to the means to get to heaven – here is the greatest division and contradiction between the religions. All religions share the same answer to this question – all except biblical Christianity. They all teach that in order to please God and achieve their various (and contradictory) promises of heaven, we must follow certain lifestyles and rules, do certain things, and act certain ways. According to them, we must 'be good' enough to outweigh our bad, in order to end up in a better place. Only the Bible disagrees with this roadmap to heaven. Only the Bible teaches that it is hopeless – **there is no way to please God** enough to earn His approval and merit heaven.

WHAT?! No way to please Him?

Nope. No way.

Only biblical Christianity teaches that:

- There is no way to earn heaven by doing enough good things,
- Not one single person has ever been good enough,
- But because God loves people anyway,
- He paid the price for our entrance into heaven Himself.

A second reason why "all religions lead to heaven" cannot be true is the extravagance of the price God paid in the sacrifice of Jesus. Consider the deeply loved, only Son of God, living together with the Father from eternity, as dear to His heart as your dear children is to your heart. And for the sake of you and me, He sent Jesus to earth, born of a virgin, living 33 years on this dirty, broken planet, rejected by the very people He wanted to save, murdered in a vile, humiliating fashion, and buried in a stone tomb. Such a price to pay for you and me!

It would be like you, loving a toy ant farm so much that you sacrificed your own child to save those 'precious' ants. I know I would never do such a thing. But God did.

But why would He conceive of, much less execute such a plan if there were already three or four other, less painful plans for salvation already in place? Why let His own Son die in such a way, if people could get to heaven in any of four different ways if they were only sincere enough? If people could get to heaven by being good enough, or by killing infidels, or by meditating on peace, or by giving to the poor – why would God go through the agony of letting His Son die? And why would He go through the trouble of getting His written Word down through the ages to us? And why would He see to it that it included statements such as Jesus is "THE way, THE truth and THE life", rather than "ANOTHER" way…? Why would Jesus say, "No man comes to the Father but through me," if there were really other ways that could do the job?

This, then, is the last reason why not all ways will get you there. Jesus Himself said that He was the only way, that the right way was narrow, and the wrong way wide. All other religions that I have researched also claim that they are the only way. Oh, sure, they will publicly claim that tolerance is good, and we should all get along. But the writings of each of the major religions claim that they are THE right one. So none of them will agree that any way is fine as long as you are peaceful and sincere. THEY CAN NOT ALL BE RIGHT!

This leaves us, still, with a decision to make. Not, "all are fine, so just pick what's best for you and be sincere", but which ONE is right? This changes the discussion to a weighing of the claims and evidence for each, and deciding which one truly is right.

I believe that an objective look at the evidence and claims of the various religions will result in the conclusion that the Bible stands head and shoulders above all others as the source of

Truth. Of course this leaves the rest as imposters, created by an evil mastermind for the purpose of leading millions of people away from God and into an eternity lost. So this evaluation and decision is very important. Not to be made lightly, for eternity depends upon it.

Chapter Thirteen – When is 'nice' not nice enough?

If Christians have a corner on relationship with God, what about all the "Nice" unsaved people?

This question gets to one of the foundational issues of salvation. Just what is it that earns a person the right to enter heaven? What do we have to do to get through the pearly gates, rather than being exiled from God's presence and condemned to the eternal flames of hell?

Another way to look at this might be, "What's a guy got to do to be right with God?" A pretty significant question, I would say.

If you've traveled with us this far in this book, you have already settled the issues of:

- Is there a God?
- Is He really involved in our lives?
- Is there evil in the world?
- Is there a heaven and a hell?

If you've answered 'no' to any of these questions, then you can skip this chapter. You've already decided that people will not spend eternity in hell, much less nice people. But if you answered 'yes' to all four, then the issue remains an important one, and we must answer the next logical question. Since there is an heaven and a hell, how do we get to enter the good place and avoid the bad one?

Most people, if you ask them how you get to go to heaven, will suggest that it is some form of a cosmic balance – at the end of each life, God piles the good things you did on one side, the bad things on the other side, and whichever way the scale tips seals your eternal fate.

In fact, every religion on earth teaches some form of this 'balancing good acts against bad acts' philosophy. Every religion except one, that is. As we mentioned before, every religion in history, excluding biblical Christianity, tries to teach its followers what they must do to earn God's approval. They all vary a bit in the details of exactly what constitutes 'good acts', but they all have a list of things to do, and another list of things to avoid doing to stay out of hell, and to get the pearly gates to swing open to let them in.

The various lists of good acts are similar in some ways. They all teach that giving to the poor, being honest and industrious, obeying your government, helping others in times of need, and praying to your god are things that earn the approval of God.

Likewise, every one of the world's religions agree on a list of activities that their god disapproves of. Stealing is bad, lying is bad, adultery is bad in most cases, and murder is bad in most cases. The items on both lists that the various religions have in common are many. And while the Bible agrees with the list of good and bad activities, the difference lies in the purpose for which good deeds are performed.

Most religions teach that good deeds are for pleasing their god, and earning entry into heaven. Biblical Christianity, however, teaches that good deeds are not done to earn entry into heaven, but are, instead, evidence of a changed life after salvation has been assured through accepting Jesus' sacrificial death as payment for one's own sins. The good works then result in rewards to be received in heaven, rather than entry into heaven.

The various non-Christian religions also differ in their descriptions of what God is like, what heaven is like, and what the ultimate goal of life is. The following outline is an extremely simplified overview of a few tenets of faith from five of the major world religions.

Who is God?

Hinduism - There are thousands of gods, with many personalities

Buddhism - There is no god

Islam - He is an unknowable, angry, capricious god

Mormonism - He is a perfected human

Biblical Christianity - One God who loves people

The goal of life?

Hinduism – Reincarnation into a better life form over and over until reaching perfection

Buddhism - Absorption into a universal consciousness - "enlightenment"

Islam – Do the will of Allah in order to achieve heaven

Mormonism - Become a god and create and populate your own universe

Biblical Christianity – Live like Christ, and accept His free gift of eternity in heaven

How do you get to heaven?

Hinduism – Do enough good works - Karma and reincarnation are methods by which man learns to do it better next time

Buddhism - Do enough good works – the eight-fold path

Islam - Do enough good works – the five pillars

Mormonism - Do enough good works – the Ten Commandments plus others

Biblical Christianity - Accept Jesus' sacrificial payment for your sins

Who is Jesus?
Hinduism - A good man

Buddhism - A good man

Islam - A prophet who did not die or resurrect

Mormonism - Another perfected human

Biblical Christianity - God's only Son – part of the trinity

What is the Bible?
Hinduism – A good book, though with errors

Buddhism - A good book, though with errors

Islam - A holy book, correct except where corrected by the Koran

Mormonism - A holy book, correct except where corrected by the Book of Mormon

Biblical Christianity – The inerrant revelation of God to humanity, inspired by Him through the writing of humans

You can see that biblical Christianity is unique among world religions in several ways:

- Its description of God as one loving God, existing as a trinity including the Father, the Son, and the Holy Spirit
- Its description of heaven or hell as the eternal destiny for every person
- Its prescription for the way to get to heaven

Christianity is the only one of the religions that teaches that there is NO WAY to please God enough by good works to earn your way into heaven! So, if the other religions are right, then nice people do not have to worry about where they will spend eternity. Their good actions as nice people will outweigh their mean actions, the scale will tip toward heaven, and in they will go to their just rewards.

If, on the other hand, the Bible is right, then each person who has ever lived, apart from Jesus Christ, has done at least one thing wrong in God's eyes, and that one 'sin' is poison enough to keep them out of heaven. The Bible teaches that even one sinful action – even one thought that is against God's perfect standard will be enough to damn the person who did it to an eternity rejected from God's presence. One little lie. One thought of lust. One theft of penny candy. One moment spent thinking bad thoughts at the guy who just cut you off in traffic. Any of these offenses committed puts a blot on your record that God can not overlook. James 10:20

Ouch! That's a tough standard to live up to. An impossible standard. Particularly when you study a bit further in to the Bible and find that it's even worse than that! The Bible teaches that every baby born on earth is the unwitting, but unfailing recipient of the sinful nature of their parents. Each perfect, cute, cuddly, innocent baby is born with the stain of sin written in their very genes – through no fault of their own, but simply because they belong to the human race. Every person descended from Adam and Eve inherits the sin trait as part of their genetic makeup. And it's a dominant gene. It always expresses itself in each life.

If the Bible is true then, nice person or not, every one of us is guilty enough to be sent to hell. In this sense, there is no person nice enough to escape the mark on their permanent record that says, "Guilty".

However, our human mind, with its logic and limited point of view says, "Nice people, trying hard to do the best they can, should not be sent to hell." But let's reframe the comment into something like this – "After all that God did to provide a free way to get right with Him again (sending us His written word, and protecting it through the ages from all attempts, human and demonic, to destroy it, coming to earth in human form and flesh to tell us Himself, and dying to pay the price for each of our mistakes) why do people still insist on thinking they have a better idea, and reject the way God provided?"

In God's economy, nice has nothing to do with salvation – only admitting that I have sinned, and accepting His payment for it will do. I look at it like this – to be assured of heaven, a person must have three knows, and one yes.

Know #1 – Know that God loves you so much that He made you perfect and unique.

Know #2 – Know that you are guilty, either by sinning sometime in your life, or by inheriting the "sin gene" that each human has.

Unfortunately, the sentence for the guilty verdict is eternal separation from God.

Know #3 – Know that God, in His love for you, paid the price for your sin by coming to earth in the flesh of a human body – known to us as Jesus Christ. Not only did He come, but He died on the cross to pay the penalty for your sin.

And the **One Yes** – Knowing these three facts is good. It's even essential. But it's not enough. Each of us must say, "Yes, God. I've sinned. And I accept your payment for my sins. I accept your gift of forgiveness, and pledge to live after your leadership rather than doing whatever suits my desires from now on."

There is nothing magical about these four steps. Yet they signify what must take place in your heart in order to find a relationship with God. According to the Bible, when you have established this sequence of knowledge AND personal acceptance of His gift of salvation, several things happen.

- You receive a new heart – one that can interact with God spirit-to-spirit. Clean and healthy and new, your new heart is alive like never before.
- You are forgiven all of your sins. They are not simply covered up, they are washed clean out of your life, and out of God's memory. Nothing you have done can come between you and Him anymore. (There may still be consequences for things you've done – crimes committed, relationships damaged, health ruined, but God will have some great things in store for you in these areas, too.)
- You receive His presence in your heart – in the form of the Holy Spirit. He will always be with you, empowering you, leading you, teaching you.

- You have access to Him every second of every day. He is willing and pleased to listen to you as you speak your heart to Him.
- You are given gifts – blessings already paid for, and awaiting your acceptance.
    - Recovered health
    - Abundant life, and your needs met
    - Abilities beyond your natural talents to use for His glory and the encouragement of other believers
    - A family of fellow Christ followers
    - Wisdom and insight into how life works
- The ability to live in such a way as to make your life count for eternity – the Bible teaches that what we do here can result in eternal rewards that we can enjoy for eternity once we get to heaven.
- Assurance that He will never leave you, and His promise that you will live forever with Him after this life is over.

This is quite a list! Particularly when you consider that all of it comes at no cost to you. It was all paid for by Christ, and given to you, conditional only on the idea that you have to accept it. No earning. No balance scales weighing your good deeds against you bad ones. No waiting until you get to the gates of heaven to find out if you merit entrance or not. The Bible is clear in telling you that when you get to heaven, when you are asked why you should get in through the gates, your only answer is, "Jesus paid for my sins."

In truth, every person on earth has had their sins paid for by the death of Jesus on the cross, and has been fully forgiven. But only those who accept that gift will receive it. Nice people and mean ones. All have been provided for. Good people or bad ones – each individual has only to open their heart in humility and accept the salvation that was been paid for long ago.

So, being nice does not earn you God's favor and friendship. This is not to say that we should not try to be nice. There are good reasons to be good to people. As I mentioned above, the Bible teaches that we get rewards in heaven for doing right here on earth. Once we are saved, everything we do for Jesus here – giving to the poor, visiting those in prison, caring for orphans and widows, being nice to people – will be remembered and rewarded in the life to come. We don't know what those rewards will be, but we are assured that we will be rewarded for living out the new good heart that we received as part of the "Salvation Package" that we got by faith in God's promises.

At the same time, those good works - giving to the poor, visiting those in prison, caring for orphans and widows, being nice to people – will do absolutely no good if we refused His offer of salvation. The 'nice' people who refused to accept God's generous gift of free salvation through faith in Jesus will look back, and with profound regret, wish that they had trusted God rather than their 'niceness'. This is one of the most profound tragedies of eternity – that people who think they are 'good enough' to merit heaven will be turned away. Matthew 7:21-22 says, "You will say, 'Lord, Lord,' and He will say 'Depart from me, for I never knew you.'"

I beg you, and God does too, don't let that be you.

Chapter Fourteen – Please God? Pulleeeese?

How does prayer work? Does prayer 'change God's mind'?

God is omniscient. He knows everything, including how every decision, every action and every word will impact the lives of the people involved in any situation. God is also good, and wants the best for people. His will for each of us is set, and He is willing to reveal it to us, either through His word or by His Spirit speaking to us.

With all of this in mind, how is it that prayer can accomplish anything? When we desire something, God already knows that we want it. He knows what is best for us. He knows what His best will is in each situation. He is known as the God who never changes – and yet the Bible contains story after story in which people ask God to do something different than what He has said, and He seems to change His mind. Examples? Glad you asked.

In Exodus 32, a story is related in which the Israelites disobey God by building a golden idol. God is ready to wipe them out and start a new nation from Moses' descendants. Moses intercedes on behalf of the people, and God spares the nation. In Genesis 18, the people of Sodom are so vile in their lifestyle that God sends angels to destroy them. But Abraham convinces God to spare them if He can find just ten righteous people in the city. Later, in First Samuel chapter eight, the nation of Israel decides that they want a king over them rather than a priest or a prophet. God says, "No," until they whine so much He decides to let them have what they want.

So whatever it is about God that never changes, it's apparently not His mind. That seems to change in some circumstances if people ask the right way, or enough times. I suggest that there are many things about God that never change – His character, His nature, His power. And in reference to our current topic, it is His will that never changes. What does change is our decision to walk in it. Because of our free will, and His decision to never force His will on us, He allows us to hear and understand His best will for us, and then still decide to reject it if we want to.

So there are times when we can ask Him for something, and in response He may tell us that it is not in our best interest to get it, and yet allow us to get it anyway. Not His perfect will, but His 'permissive" will. And the result of getting this less than perfect will is always less than our lives could have been if we had more closely followed the Designer's best plan for us. He knows best, but allows us to choose second best, or third best, or out-and-out sin if we set our minds on it.

In another sense, prayer has impact on our lives in other ways, too. What we refer to as prayer may be both simpler and more 'partitioned' than we first think. Literally, prayer means talking with God. A pretty simple concept, and God loves for us to do it. He wants us to fellowship with Him, and to spend time in His presence – pouring our heart out to Him, and taking time to listen. That's why Jesus died, after all, to purchase a way for us to return to that fellowship.

However, we could also look at prayer as three distinct types of interactions with Him – commanding problems to be resolved, claiming gifts that He offers us, and simple fellowship with Him. Let's discuss each of these a bit.

1) **Commanding** – When faced with an attack by Satan, an attempt by him to kill, steal or destroy our lives, we are given authority to 'speak to the mountain'. We are authorized and empowered to speak directly to the problem and command it, with the authority given to us by Jesus, to get out of our lives. This would include common life challenges such as:
    a. Sickness – Just as Jesus spoke to the fever that was afflicting Peter's mother-in-law, we are authorized to command sickness to leave. (My book, The Rest of the Gospel, goes into this in more detail.)
    b. Poverty – When He came to earth from heaven, Jesus became poor so that we might become rich. When we have missed God's leading in areas that have led us into slavery to debt, we can repent of those mistakes, and then command debt to leave.
    c. Demonic influence, attack or stronghold – Just as Jesus cast out 'Legion' from the man near the tombs, we have been given authority over every spiritual attack or stronghold. Satan has no authority over us other than what we give to him, and no ability to resist our command when we, the righteous redeemed, speak in Jesus' name.

Another way to look at these modes of battle against Satan's plans involves the words 'bind' and 'resist'. We are authorized and ordered to use these modes of power encounters against the various attacks of the evil one. We are to use verbal commands in the name of the Lord Jesus Christ to resist and bind Satan's plans, his power, his intentions, his attacks. These are examples of speaking to the problem with authority to use the power given to us by God. It's His power. He has given us authority to use it. (John 14:12)

2) When we find ourselves in need of something that Jesus purchased for us during His time here on earth, we are authorized to come and receive it. **Claiming a promise** offered to us is not presumptuous. Rather, it is expected as loved children coming to a good father who longs to give good things. We can, with full assurance and boldness, learn of the promises made by Him, and claim them for ourselves in areas such as:
    a. Salvation – whosoever will may receive His prepaid gift of salvation. Revelation 22:17
    b. Health – by His stripes we were healed, and all who touched Him were healed. 1 Peter 2:24, and Matthew 8:16
    c. Prosperity – He became poor so that we might become rich. 2 Corinthians 8:9
    d. Protection – a thousand may fall at my side… but it will not come near me. Psalm 91, Revelation 6:11
    e. Leading – He makes the crooked path straight. Proverbs 3:5
    f. Wisdom – He gives to all liberally, when we ask without wavering. James 1:5-6
    g. Forgiveness – When we confess, He forgives – 1 John 1:9

These are times when, once we know what has been purchased by Christ for us, (See Substitutions and Examples in Chapter 5 of The Rest of the Gospel) and once we believe in our heart what He said in His written word, we can boldly receive them, or grab hold of them by faith. We no longer need to beg Him for these things, but may receive them by faith. And when Satan comes again to try to convince us otherwise, we must speak the word aloud, and cling all the tighter to what is ours. This is believing and receiving.

Faith, of course, is the biggest five-letter word in the English language. Much misused, and often misunderstood. Faith is not merely wishing for a good thing, nor is it merely believing strongly enough to get something we want. Faith is actually acting on something we know to be true, based on a credible source, even when we cannot see it, touch it, or measure it. Like God, we believe and therefore we speak. We speak those things which are not as though they are.

Of course there is no more credible source than the written Word of God! We can be fully assured that what He has told us in it is true. More true than our five senses. More true than any report of man. When we are told that He has purchased our healing, our protection, our salvation – we can bank on it, and thank Him for it even before it shows up in our flesh. When His word tells us that we will have our needs met, that He will lead us, and that He will give us wisdom for any situation – we can relax, sleep in peace, and look forward to the manifestation of that truth. This bears repeating, we no longer have to beg Him for these things, but must only receive them by faith.

3) And then there are times when we just need to **be in His presence** and share our hearts with Him. This is a combination of seeking His face, basking in His Word, and listening for the still small voice as He gives light to

our path. This is where true worshippers come "in spirit and in truth" to simply bow and honor Him in private. These are times of resting, of growing our faith by meditating on, or speaking His word aloud to ourselves. This is where we get to share our dreams and desires with Him, and then trust Him to, "... do exceeding abundantly above all that we ask or think, according to the power that works in us," (Ephesians 3:20) This is where we learn what His best will is for our situations, and decide to follow it, by His grace, no matter what our flesh wants.

So prayer is not begging God for things. It is not asking Him over and over in an effort to wear Him down. It is not an attempt to pry good things out of the stingy hand of Almighty God. It is not proving how deserving we are by persisting in prayer.

Prayer may then include:

- Receiving through faith what He has already offered, or
- Using the authority given to us by Christ to command bad things out of our lives, or
- Quietly sharing with and listening to our loving Father.

Speaking to the problems we face, believing and receiving what He has already purchased for us, or quietly sharing our heart of hearts in fellowship with Him. These are the prerogatives of the child of God!

Of course, faith is a key component of all three of these portions of prayer. Faith, again, is acting on a truth that has been given by a credible source, even if we cannot see, feel or measure that truth at the time. Faith is believing that His promises, given in His Word, are more real than what our eyes see.

The spoken Word is a second key component to effective, powerful prayer, since it is with the heart that we believe, yet with the mouth that we confess truth and receive it. So speak up – audibly – in order to enjoy spiritual impact in this physical world. (Again, for a more in-depth discussion of the power of our spoken words, look for the chapter on that topic in The Rest of the Gospel.)

Again, here in the matter of effective prayer, just as in so many other areas of our spiritual life, the spoken word is critical. Don't hesitate to speak aloud in all three areas of prayer, even if you are by yourself. Confession is "agreeing with what He says about any given topic." When we speak the Truth that we find in His written Word aloud, things around us change. This is powerful and effective prayer.

Chapter Fifteen – Nothing up my sleeve!

How does the spiritual world impact the physical?

This is a fascinating topic, but one that may require some speculation – extrapolation based on what we can glean from the Word. Is it 'kosher' to do so? To take revealed truth and then consider what might be true beyond it? Perhaps, but with two conditions:

1) That the extrapolation does not contradict any other truth, particularly biblical Truth, and
2) That the extrapolation does not lead people to confusion, or other action that is ungodly

It is clear that the spiritual world does impact the physical realm from numerous examples in the Bible. Angels destroyed armies in the ancient Jewish wars against the people living in the promised land. Three Jewish wise men were saved from the middle of a deadly fire in Babylon. Storms were calmed using spiritual authority. A virgin gave birth. And men were healed from incurable diseases. What we see and touch was originally created by God's Spirit forming matter using only the power of His spoken Word.

Then there is the evil side of spiritual interaction with the material. The biblical record tells us that many angels, spirit beings themselves, were cast to the earth after they rebelled against God's rule. They then interacted with mankind in many situations – Satan tempted Eve, demons seduced women to produce a species of giants, demons dwelt within people causing aberrant behavior, evil spirits brought temptations to the minds of men and women.

In opposition to these, the Holy Spirit of God brings conviction to men's hearts, and God's servant-angels have appeared on earth to win battles, to stop various people's progress down a wrong path, to show a better path, to explain God's plan in specific situations, and more.

Biblical examples go on and on. And in modern days we still see people healed, wisdom granted, lives changed and renewed, prayers answered. Angels continue to intervene in our affairs, protecting and ministering God's will to God's children.

So how does this happen? How does a spiritual event impact or influence our material world? Spiritual beings and spiritual power do impact physical life in at least four ways – sometimes in direct interaction, but more consistently in subtle manners.

1) God Himself speaks and acts as a spiritual being, impacting, creating and sustaining all we see. His trustworthy word, empowered by His complete faith, brings that which is not yet materially manifest into being.
2) Angels and demons appear in bodily form:
    a. In the old testament angels appeared to Abraham, and demons interacted with human women to produce the race called the Nephilim.
    b. In the New Testament angels appeared to shepherds and others, and we are still admonished to treat strangers kindly, since they could be angels in disguise.

3) The battle field of the mind – When spiritual forces influence the soul of a person, they may influence a person to make decisions that can impact their physical actions and their health. This is called demonic influence or oppression. If a person gives their decisions, actions and will entirely over to that demon's influence, the spirit will take deeper control of the mind. This is called demonic possession.
4) Genetic influence – Another aspect of this, which may impact any person's situation, is the matter of genetic predisposition to illness. This relates to the culmination of circumstances in which our parents or grandparents lost battles to temptation, losing ground to Satan and giving him an opportunity to attack through genetic lines. When this happens, we pay a price for "generational curses" that can be broken and healed (just like any disease can be). But if they are not dealt with, they will cause problems as those generational curses lead to changes in genetic makeup, leading, in time, to diseases which are an expression of those genetic changes. In this way, the demonic oppression or possession takes advantage of an opportunity to actually change DNA strands in such a way as to impact that person's physical health.

Granted, this is speculative. But such a chain of events – spiritual impact leading to genetic changes followed by physical expression – could explain how such things as addictions, family tendencies, lifestyle choices, etc. could begin, and then be handed down from generation to generation.

It is true that the spiritual world does impact what we see, hear and feel on the physical plane. In fact, the Bible teaches that the spiritual realm is more solid and 'real' than the physical realm feels, and that spiritual laws dictate and enforce physical laws.

The physical world seems more real to us merely because we are trapped in the four dimensions that contain the physical world. When we are eventually released from the constraints of these four dimensions, it will become suddenly clear to us just what is real and what is insubstantial. The human mind probably cannot imagine all the ways in which the heaven experience will exceed the earth experience, but perhaps, without those constraints, we will finally be able to touch colors, hear tastes, and taste thoughts. Certainly we will be able to think more clearly and creatively than we ever could in our finest earth-bound moments. We will finally experience the universe as it was created to be experienced. And what we sense as the physical world will be immersed in, and completed by the rest of the created realm.

For now, we know that the physical realm is touched and changed by the spiritual realm when God wills it so, when an individual exercises faith in grasping a godly promise, or when a person surrenders their will to Satan's plans. Make no mistake, our thoughts, choices and words impact more than simply what we see with our physical eyes.

Chapter Sixteen – The bent balance.

Why do bad things happen to good people?

For that matter, why do good things happen to bad people? We see it all the time – the bully of the block (or the bully/leader of a nation) bent on having his own way, seems to get his own way – often from walking over the broken bodies and shattered lives of those he misuses. The leader of a successful business seems to flourish at the expense of his underpaid, over-worked employees. A drug lord lives large – thanks to the dollars gathered from the addicts he helped to enslave.

On the other hand, the extremely nice gentleman who mows the neighbor's lawn, and greets you with a cheery hello every time you see him, develops cancer. A lovely family of four is struck by a drunk driver in an auto accident in which three are killed and the mother left paralyzed. A country is invaded, and a whole peaceful people group is targeted for ethnic cleansing. On and on, we hear of tragedies experienced by nice people. And our heart cries out, "Why?"

This is certainly not a new question. The Bible records the question asked of a blind man – "Whose fault is it?" and of the victims of a construction accident – "What did they do to deserve this?" (John 9:2)

In response, Jesus tells us that it is not necessarily because of direct sin/consequence relationship that people suffer, though that certainly can happen. But the answer is as complex as the world in which we live. And the same factors that we have discussed in earlier chapters will bear strongly in the discussion.

Recall that God designed this world with 'wild cards' in the deck. By 'wild cards' I do not mean random occurrences, for surely God does not throw dice to decide the fate of the people He created out of a motive of love, and whom He continues to love. No, the wild cards are two factors that impact the execution of His perfect will – the existence of Satan, and the free will of people who can, because of their free will, decide to love and follow Him, or to turn from God, reject His plan, and choose their own path.

So why do bad things happen to good people? There are several reasons. Several sources of bad events.

First, Satan, a truly evil being, looks for opportunities to "steal, kill, and destroy". He tries to mess up lives for several reasons that I can come up with, and there are probably more.

1) If Satan can fill a life with tragedy, there is a chance that the afflicted person will blame God. If Satan can do the damage subtly, with a smoke screen or distance between the tragic event and himself, the victims may say, "If God did this to me, I want nothing to do with Him." And Satan has done a brilliant job of setting the stage for this misplaced blame. He acts quietly rather than overtly – never coming out so strong that people will look and see that it is obviously him at work. No, it would tip his hand if he showed up in all his obvious evil. In fact, he is said to be able to "appear as an angel of light", seeming good as he works his malevolence. He then nudges the victims' minds to look accusingly at God, point their finger, and cry, "How could You?" People who are caught up in blaming God will not be likely to trust Him for their eternal destiny.

2) If Satan can bring tragedy, he may be able to derail that person's desire from doing good to others. When we are so caught up in our own pain, it can be difficult to summon the energy and good will to do good to others. More upset, suffering, short-tempered people – that's right up Satan's alley.
3) From the day he was cast out of heaven for rebelling against God, Satan has delighted in destroying God's creation. Anything God likes, Satan is against. On top of this, Satan knows that God intends to send him to hell eventually. He desires to take as many with him as possible.

Second, not all bad is caused by Satan. Sometimes he has nothing to do with it. And even without his conniving assistance, there is plenty of opportunity for people to 'step in it'. For even 'good' people live less than perfect lives. Some of the life-decisions good people make have consequences. For instance, a good person may smoke cigarettes leading to cancer. A nice man may have a tendency to drive too fast, or while sleepy, leading to an accident.

Third, while God desires His people to live peaceably and prosperously, there are times when His people step away from His leading and protection – either in outright sin, or in making decisions that leave them open to harmful events. For instance, God might warn a person to stay home rather than travelling on a vacation. If the person fails to heed that warning, and goes to the beach anyway, they may blissfully travel, only to be caught up in a storm. Perhaps an otherwise good person is considering an investment. She ignores the warning of the Holy Spirit, to stay away from it, and loses her life savings, ending up in poverty.

In each of these examples, however, God has promised that, even if the event is bad and outside of His best will for the individual, He will work it out for good. One of the amazing things about God's wisdom and power is His ability to take events that deviate from His best will, and use them for good. (See Romans 8:28) What a comfort to rest in the knowledge of His unending goodness. The consequences of missing His will may be painful, but will end up for the good of those who love Him, and for His glory in the end.

How about good things happening to bad people? Again, there are at least a couple potential reasons.

1) Satan, being the clever hellion that he is, is a master of deceit. And he has had thousands of years to practice his wily plots. He has experimented, tested and honed his lies. He has tried, and improved on, his skills at leading people away from a relationship with the Creator. He may see a person who has chosen to ignore God, and who is, as a result, not going to end up in heaven. Satan, at all costs, desires to keep people from heaven. So he could conceivably find it helpful to his goals to nudge events in such a way as to make this unsaved, evil person rich and comfortable, for rich and comfortable people have less reason to feel a need to seek God. "Life is good! Who needs to clutter it up with God?"

2) God's rules for the universe work for everyone. So if a bad person obeys God's laws for affluence, they may be affluent – even if they break other laws.

Know two things regarding the worldly success of bad people. Though they seem to flourish, we are warned in the Word first not to envy them their brief successes, and second that they will answer for their evil in the end.

Chapter Seventeen – Why does it matter, anyway?

Think of your life as a story that you get to write. You, the main character in your story, get to make decisions about what you will do, how you will react, how you will spend your time. This frame of reference was crystallized for me in a book by Donald Miller, called "A Million Miles in a Thousand Years." I highly recommend it as a way to change your thinking about what you are doing with your life.

One of the keys to a good story is that the characters in it must know what they want, and what they will do to get it – even in the face of difficulties they must overcome to achieve their goal.

Of course, the bigger the objective of their striving, the better the story. The greater the hurdles that must be overcome, the better the story, too. If the worthy goal requires great risks, that makes the story grander.

Thinking about your own life as a story changes mere "Goal Setting" into the possibility of leaving a legacy at the end of your life. It switches the mundane and boring day after day chore of getting a paycheck to get food and pay your rent and buy a bigger TV, into the adventure and challenge of making your life count. Consider the parable of three men digging a ditch A passerby stops to talk to them, asking each one, "What are you doing?" The first laborer growls his answer, "Obviously, I'm digging this stupid ditch so I can get paid. I can't wait for the weekend so I can get my money and go to the bar." The second man answers, "I'm working hard to earn enough money to buy groceries for my wife and kids." And the third man replies with a smile, "I'm helping to build the foundation of a new hospital that will save the lives of thousands in years to come." And this is what life is meant to be! Our lives should matter!

Take a moment and evaluate your life as if it were a story you were reading, or a riveting story you were watching in movie format. Is it an epic saga? Or is it just another boring story? However the first chapters of your life may have read, as the author of your own story, you now have a chance to make the rest of your story interesting, empowering, daring and worthwhile. Or you can coast from concert to sports event to reality TV show, to yet another dinner out. Create, invest and participate, or observe, coast and take. Your life – your choice.

To make your life worth 'reading', you must pick a goal – a worthwhile thing that you will endeavor to achieve. Then, keeping that goal in mind, decide how you are going to spend your next hour. Then the next one. Then the next one... Does the use of that hour advance you toward your goal or not?

This is important "front of mind" stuff, for indeed, our lives do matter. The good things and the difficult that happen in the pages of our own stories matter. Sure, struggles go on, but we are promised that God will work even the worst things into good outcomes. We are promised that Jesus defeated Satan and then handed authority to live in that victory over to us. We are assured that He intends for us to have an abundant life.

Certainly, there will be challenges in this adventure. Challenges in listening for God's leading when the world is clamoring for our attention. Challenges as Satan takes shots at us in his attempts to undermine our usefulness to God. And there will be challenges as we encounter the other thing God's Word promises us along with the abundant life – persecution.

Yes, we are promised persecution – the attacks of Satan channeled through the offices of people who hate Christ and everything pertaining to Him. Even when we follow God closely, obey Him completely, and live a life that is a witness for Him, Satan will continue trying to attack us.

Not that there is a difference between, on the one hand:

- Missing God's leading and ending up in trouble because we make bad decisions
- Sinning and ending up in trouble as a consequence of our sinful decision, and
- Satan attacking through the gaps in our hedge of protection caused by these life-errors

And on the other hand:

- Being persecuted for living a godly life of active service for God.

For some reason, in His perfect wisdom, God has seen that those of us who live for Him will have persecution. We will be attacked simply for being Christ followers. We will be slandered, lied about, hated, arrested, abused, beaten, imprisoned, and killed simply for refusing to compromise our testimony for Jesus. In fact, since the inception of the Way of Christ at His crucifixion, His followers have been persecuted in every century and in every country. While we in the United States have been insulated from it in recent decades, more people were killed for His cause in the 20th century than in any century before.

Yet, in spite of this, the Bible teaches us the great truth that our actions positively impact eternity in several ways. In fact, it can be seen that because of this persecution, our lives matter.

History shows over and over, that His church as a body grows faster and stronger during times of persecution than in times of peace and acceptance. But in either case, in peace or in persecution, our individual, unique lives matter.

They matter to us now. They matter to us for eternal outcomes. And they matter to those watching us live out our answers to these sticky questions.

Conclusion

We have spent 17 chapters, spread over 120 pages, discussing some sticky, difficult questions. We have suggested 17 answers that are as strong and flexible as carbon fiber. One way to look at these questions is to group them into two categories – ten questions that have clear biblical answers, and seven that have answers that are 'softer', in that they are merely extrapolations and opinions derived from what I have learned over the course of 40 years of walking with God and reading His Word.

The questions are undeniably hard – diamond hard. People have grappled with them for all of the history of mankind. The answers are strong too – strong but flexible. They have room to give a bit when we wrestle with them, but they stand up under logical and biblical scrutiny. I do not presume to present them as the final answer. They are not words from God like the scriptures are. They just make sense to me, without contradicting the written Word. So perhaps they will be helpful to you, also.

But, even with answers that seem to work, there comes a point in some of these questions, discussions and answers at which we have to sit back, sigh, and say, "I really don't know." There comes a time in dealing with such root issues at which we need to finally, and simply, trust God. For in spite of all our learning and striving for understanding, we all will agree that the sum total of our knowledge is a mere fraction of the total cosmic 'book' of knowledge in the universe. And knowing this limit to our knowledge and understanding – even when we pride ourselves in the smug feeling of knowing some things – we must admit that amidst the vast repository of still-unperceived knowledge outside of our own, there may be pieces of knowledge and wisdom that make sense of the mysteries. Those things about which we just can't understand "why God did that" may make sense when seen from the point of view of Him who really does know everything.

We must, in the end, trust that He knows better than we do, that He is truly good and fair, that His ways and thoughts are deeper and higher and wider than ours are, that we really may not know or understand as much or as fully as He does. And at that point – when we find ourselves trusting this God – we can relax.

It is important that we arrive at the point where we trust Him with these questions – because we may not ever truly know what the answers are. But we will never go wrong in assuming that God is on our side, and that He is good.

The man named Job, several thousand years ago, asked some of these same questions, and wrestled verbally with God through 40 of his own chapters. He heard God stop him in his mental tracks, and he came away saying that he still didn't understand, but that he would trust his God to the end anyway. In fact, God talked directly to Job for several of those chapters, and even with all of Job's initial questions and accusations, God never did come right out and tell Job why those calamities happened to him.

The questions are undeniably hard. The answers are, by necessity, flexible. When we get to heaven, perhaps it will be made clear to us. On the other hand at that point, with all of heaven's wonders available to us, and seeing the Father face-to-face, the importance of these questions may fade. In the light of

His presence, the desperate need for answers will bow to awe at His holiness and grace.

While we are here, however, these questions weigh on us. Unless we are in denial of these issues and how they impact our lives, they show up every day in response to broken relationships, during hopeless-feeling illnesses, in the quiet, achy desire for something beyond the daily routines we are wrapped up in. The questions usually tug at us in quiet yearnings, but occasionally crescendo to attention-grabbing shouts for answers.

It is a truth that God is calling out for us to know Him better. I think it was C. S. Lewis who shared his opinion that God whispers to us through the wonders of nature. He speaks to us in His written Word. And sometimes He shouts to get our attention in the painful times of life. In examining these 18 sticky questions I have concluded that the ultimate purpose of life for each of us is to simply know and walk with God. The tough questions are left in life to encourage us to do just that, and it seems that facing these questions, and the circumstances in life that force us to ask them, drives us to either draw close to Him or to curse Him. Which way any of us chooses – draw close, or curse – is largely dependent on how we answer the seventeen questions. It is a choice between trusting Him or turning from Him. Steady faith, or a shaken fist.

Other than knowing God as a personal, caring being, what may be even more important than the final answers to these other questions is the fact that we seek answers from Him. And that we continue seeking them, even when we don't understand.

When I can't see – I'll believe
When I don't understand – I'll obey
When I don't hear – I'll still listen
When I can't find You – I will worship
(From 'I Will Worship')

Made in the USA
Charleston, SC
17 December 2012